MOUNTAIN
AND
WILDERNESS

MOUNTAIN AND WILDERNESS

Prayer and Worship in the Biblical World and Early Church

Paul T. Coke

A CROSSROAD BOOK
The Seabury Press • New York

1978
The Seabury Press
815 Second Avenue
New York, N.Y. 10017

Printed in the United States of America

Library of Congress Cataloging in Publication Data

Coke, Paul T   1933–
The mountain and the wilderness.
"A Crossroad book."
Bibliography: p.
1.Worship—History. 2.Prayer—History.   I.Title.
BL550.C64   264'.009'01   77–16154
ISBN 0–8164–2177–3

CONTENTS

INTRODUCTION   1
ACKNOWLEDGEMENTS   5

I   WORSHIP IN ANCIENT GREECE   7

The New Testament was written in the Greek
language and its proclamation was directed to
Greek-speaking audiences. Prayer and worship
were vital parts of ancient Greek civilization.
Thus, to appreciate more fully the meaning of
prayer and the richness of worship in the New
Testament, we begin with some reflections upon
the heritage · and background Greek culture
brought to the message of the Bible.

II ABRAHAM AND MOSES
    IN THE WORSHIP OF ISRAEL   26

A New Testament presupposes an Old Testament. The life and teaching of Jesus stand in
constant relationship to his compatriots, their

history, and their traditions. To begin to understand Jesus' unique qualities we must start with the faith of Israel and the Holy Scriptures of the people of God.

III THE PRAYERS OF DAVID AND SOLOMON   45

The Old Testament has two treasure houses for prayer and worship, the Psalter and the teachings of the wise men of Israel. The writers of the New Testament were more influenced by the Psalms of David than by any other book in the Old Testament. And Solomon inaugurated the temple worship which provided the setting for both the beginning and end of Jesus' life, as well as the location and point of departure for much of his teaching. Our attention is therefore devoted to the worship and beliefs associated with David and Solomon.

IV THE MOUNT OF TRANSFIGURATION AND THE WILDERNESS OF TEMPTATION   66

The importance of prayer in Jesus' own life and ministry is especially emphasized in the Gospel of Luke, which begins and ends in Jerusalem with prayer in the temple. Matthew records Jesus' Sermon on the Mount, with his teaching about prayer and the most complete statement we have of the Lord's Prayer. Thus the two evangelists present us with unique insights into the meaning of prayer for Jesus.

V THE OLD TEMPLE
AND THE NEW SPIRIT OF PRAYER 85

With the rise of the Christian Church, the centuries-old worship in Jerusalem came to be understood in a new light. The resurrection of Jesus and the presence of his Spirit with his disciples, wherever and whoever they were, marked the end of the temple as a unique inspiration point and mount of revelation and prayer. The seeming wilderness of the Gentiles was to bloom as the Spirit of Jesus brought blessing to the accursed foreigners, forgiveness to the outcasts, and joy to every person who would receive it.

VI THE ADVANCE OF CHRISTIAN FAITH
AND WORSHIP IN THE WEST AND IN
THE EAST 110

Both Acts and the Epistles of Paul show the ongoing movement of the Christian Church from Jerusalem to Rome. In the following generations of discipleship and worship, this advance continued as the young faith matured and bore much fruit. Indeed the wilderness of temptation and the desert of our fear became inspiration points as the Spirit of Christ continued to transform the whole world.

NOTES AND SUGGESTIONS FOR FURTHER
READING 137

INTRODUCTION

Worship is an expression of thankfulness and reverence for the Creator; prayer is an effort to articulate in language our communion with God.

Our working definition is brief. It only points toward the unlimited wealth of the religious experience and the heritage of mankind. This book is a first step into that rich world of faith. It attempts to offer a brief introduction to the prayer and worship of Greece and Israel, in the ministry of Jesus, and in the ongoing mission of the first centuries of the Christian Church. In chapter one we begin with Greece because the New Testament was written in Greek and its language about prayer presupposes many of the religious traditions of ancient Greece. In chapters two and three we move on to the Old Testament, which served as Holy Scripture for the early Church, and provided most of the models of prayer and worship used by Jesus and his disciples as their starting points. The next two chapters continue exploration of our theme, the mountain of prayer and the heights of worship, in contrast to the wilderness of temptation and the lowlands of despair, with illustrations from the life of Jesus, Peter, and Paul. Finally chapter six shows the important transition from the experience of the early Church, as seen in the New Testament, to that of the earliest writers on prayer and worship after the biblical Scriptures were completed.

The book is designed for individual or group study. The individual reader can complete the six chapters at his own pace and, if interested, follow up the suggestions for further reflection and discussion at the end of each chapter. There is also an optional Lenten study guide for persons who may like to relate the themes of each chapter to the corresponding Collect in Lent from The Proposed Book of Common Prayer of the Episcopal Church. These historic prayers are part of the glorious heritage of all Christians, and are increasingly to be found in new liturgies and worship books, both Catholic and Protestant. It may be that the individual reader might wish to converse or correspond with a friend about some of these topics. The book will have served its purpose well if it becomes an occasion and springboard for deeper meditation and serious reflection upon the themes it presents.

It is hoped, however, that the book may also be of assistance to discussion groups and circles of friends wishing to widen their understanding of prayer and worship. Often during the six weeks of Lent, for example, churches have special programs of weekly study and discussion. The six chapters of this work are designed to help meet this interest. If a chapter is read ahead of each meeting by every member of the group, then perhaps one person could make a fifteen-minute summary and response to the chapter, and other members could be responsible for initiating conversation about the suggested topics for discussion and about other items of interest to the group, stimulated by each chapter as the group studies the theme of the mountain of prayer and the heights of worship—points of inspiration from the past for faith today.

ACKNOWLEDGEMENTS

This book has grown out of courses taught at the Seminario Episcopal del Caribe in Puerto Rico and the Episcopal Theological Seminary of the Southwest in Austin, Texas. I am much indebted to my students and colleagues for their interest and stimulation. A senior seminarian, Mr. Kenneth Barker, my mother, Mrs. Beatrice Coke, and an editor of The Seabury Press, Mr. William Gentz, have read the first draft of this work, and their suggestions have been very valuable and much appreciated. Biblical citations, unless otherwise indicated, are from the Revised Standard Version of the Bible and Apocrypha, copyrighted 1946, 1952, © 1971, 1973, used with permission. Finally, I am most indebted to my family for the time and encouragement to write this study, which is dedicated to my wife, truly my *sine qua non*.

I

WORSHIP IN ANCIENT GREECE

THE VISION FROM DELPHI

When you reach the top of the hot, dry hills after the long, twisting roads from Athens to Delphi, you find cool olive groves, a brilliantly blue sky, and the glistening temples of Apollo and the other ancient Greek gods. And shimmering far below is the distant gulf of Corinth. It seems easier in Delphi to glimpse the eternal in all the change and confusion of ordinary life, to hear the voice of timeless reason instead of the chaotic babble of many voices below.[1] It was to these mountains some twenty-four hundred years ago that a young man came to seek inspiration from the god Apollo. Chaerephon was his name; and he had a friend whom he could not understand, yet whose words were unforgettable and penetratingly true. This friend was Socrates, and time and time again Socrates claimed that he really did not know anything at all and that the best he could do was to ask questions in his search for the truth. Yet those questions seemed to bring Chaerephon and others to remarkable new insight and self-knowledge.

So it was to the temple that celebrated self-knowledge

that Chaerephon went, for over the door of Apollo's temple was inscribed the challenge: "Know thyself." Here, on the holy mountain of Delphi, Chaerephon came to try to decide if his friendship with Socrates and his attention to his puzzling questions were worthwhile. At Apollo's temple Chaerephon asked the priestess of the shrine whether there was anyone wiser than Socrates. The priestess replied that there was no one.

We have a description of Socrates' amazed response to the extraordinary praise given him on Delphi, that he was the wisest man in the world:

> After puzzling about it for some time, I set myself at last with considerable reluctance to check the truth of it in the following way. I went to interview a man with a high reputation for wisdom, because I felt that here if anywhere I should succeed in disproving the oracle and pointing out to my divine authority "You said that I was the wisest of men, but here is a man who is wiser than I am."
>
> Well, I gave a thorough examination to this person— I need not mention his name, but it was one of our politicians that I was studying when I had this experience —and in conversation with him I formed the impression that although in many people's opinion, and especially in his own, he appeared to be wise, in fact he was not. Then when I began to try to show him that he only thought he was wise and was not really so, my efforts were resented both by him and by many of the other people present. However, I reflected as I walked away: "Well, I am certainly wiser than this man. It is only too likely that neither of us has any knowledge to boast of; but he thinks that he knows something which he does not know, whereas I am quite conscious of my ignorance. At any rate it seems

that I am wiser than he is to this small extent, that I do
not think that I know what I do not know. . . ."

From that time on I interviewed one person after another. I realized with distress and alarm that I was making
myself unpopular, but I felt compelled to put my religious duty first; since I was trying to find out the meaning
of the oracle. . . . I want you to think of my adventures
as a sort of pilgrimage undertaken to establish the truth
of the oracle once for all. . . . The truth of the matter,
gentlemen, is pretty certainly this: that real wisdom is the
property of God, and this oracle is his way of telling us
that human wisdom has little or no value. It seems to me
that he is not referring literally to Socrates, but has
merely taken my name as an example, as if he would say
to us "The wisest of you men is he who has realized,
like Socrates, that in respect of wisdom he is really
worthless."

That is why I still go about seeking and searching in
obedience to the divine command, if I think that anyone
is wise, whether citizen or stranger; and when I think that
any person is not wise, I try to help the cause of God by
proving that he is not. This occupation has kept me too
busy to do much either in politics or in my own affairs;
in fact, my service to God has reduced me to extreme
poverty.[2]

Indeed Socrates was the wisest of his generation, simply
because he could recognize his own ignorance and his dependence upon the Divine for illumination and clarity. The
so-called wise men of his time thought that they knew all
the answers; Socrates tried instead to find the right questions to ask in his "pilgrimage" truly to know himself.

Socrates' quest for self-knowledge and pursuit of the
truth, wherever it might lead him, cost him his life, for the
government of Athens thought that his many questions

9

were subversive. Although threatened by the authorities of his city, Socrates refused to abandon his embarrassing questions and seemingly unpatriotic activities because he believed that an inner spirit from God himself called and impelled him to his life of philosophy, literally the love of the divine wisdom, no matter what it cost him. Shortly before he was executed, Socrates told his critics:

> When I was ordered by the Generals whom you, O men of Athens, chose to command me, at Potidaea and Amphipolis and Delium, I remained where they placed me, like any other man, facing death; strange, indeed, would be my conduct, if now, when . . . God orders me to fulfil the philosopher's mission of searching into myself and other men, I were to desert my post through fear of death, or any other fear. . . . For the fear of death is indeed the pretence of wisdom and not real wisdom, being a pretence of knowing the unknown; and no one knows whether death, which men in their fear apprehend to be the greatest evil, may not be the greatest good. Is not this ignorance of a disgraceful sort, the ignorance which is the conceit that a man knows what he does not know? And in this respect only I believe myself to differ from men in general, and may perhaps claim to be wiser than they are—that whereas I know but little of the world below, I do not suppose that I know: but I do know that injustice and disobedience to a better, whether God or man, is evil. . . . Men of Athens, I honor and love you; but I shall obey God rather than you.[3]

Two qualities are especially impressive in Socrates' lifestyle and vocation. First, his individualism and sense of personal integrity is remarkable. Although he loved political life and social intercourse, the gossip of the marketplace and the conviviality of a dinner party, Socrates was always his own man, fearless in speaking the truth as he saw it and honestly differing from nearly everyone he spoke to. The dialogues of Plato are an eloquent and timeless monument to the "Socratic method" of question and answer among friends and adversaries, concerned only to get at the truth.

In Plato's dialogue, the *Republic,* Book VII, there is an illustration of the philosopher's task, which seems very close to Socrates' personal vocation. It is almost a self-portrait. We are asked to imagine an underground chamber in which people have been chained from their childhood and can only see shadows thrown in front of them on the dark walls of the cave from a fire burning behind them:

> Suppose one of them were let loose, and suddenly compelled to stand up and turn his head and look and walk towards the fire; all these actions would be painful and he would be too dazzled to see properly the objects of which he used to see the shadows. So if he was told that what he used to see was mere illusion and that he was now nearer reality and seeing more correctly, because he was turned towards objects that were more real, and if on top of that he were compelled to say what each of the passing objects was when it was pointed out to him, don't you think he would be at a loss, and think that what he used to see was more real than the objects now being pointed out to him? . . . And if he were . . . forcibly dragged up the steep and rocky ascent and not let go till he had been dragged out into the sunlight, the process would be a painful one, to which he would much object, and when he emerged into the light his eyes would be . . . overwhelmed by the brightness. . . . First he would find it easiest to look at shadows, next at the reflections of men and other objects in water, and later on at the

11

> objects themselves. . . . The thing he would be able to do
> last would be to look directly at the sun, and observe its
> nature without using reflections in water or any other
> medium, but just as it is. . . . Then what do you think
> would happen . . . if he went back to sit in his old seat in
> the cave? Wouldn't his eyes be blinded by the darkness,
> because he had come in suddenly out of the daylight?
> . . . And if he had to discriminate between the shadows,
> in competition with the other prisoners, while he was still
> blinded and before his eyes got used to the darkness—
> a process that might take some time—wouldn't he be
> likely to make a fool of himself? And they would say that
> his visit to the upper world had ruined his sight, and that
> the ascent was not worth even attempting. And if anyone
> tried to release them and lead them up, they would kill
> him if they could lay hands on him.[4]

The story illustrates Socrates' own experience of vocation,
feeling driven from this world of shadows, mere appear-
ances, and fleeting illusions to the real world above of
eternal truth.

But having been led to a vision of the good, the philosopher, who represents every honest man, is compelled by
goodness itself never to remain contentedly in the warm
sunshine of his personal experiences of illumination and
insight; he must return to his companions in the dark cave
and try to share his new understanding of the truth, even
though he runs the risk of being despised and even condemned by his former friends. Socrates' strong individualism and sense of personal integrity is thus balanced by an
equally serious commitment to his city and to his fellow
citizens. The God whose inner guiding he followed to the
heights of speculation and reflection always led him back to

his home town to be with others—a second impressive quality of Socrates.

Some of the prayers attributed to Socrates and his companions illustrate very well this equilibrium between individual integrity and communal responsibility. In the dialogue entitled the *Phaedrus,* Socrates and his friend arrive at the banks of the river Ilissus at Athens, and he asks, "Will it not be proper to pray to the gods here before we go?" The companion replies, "What else should we do?" and Socrates prays:

> O beloved Pan and all ye gods in this place, grant to me beauty in the inward man, and may all that I possess be in accord thereto. May I reckon rich the wise man only. May that store of gold be mine which none but the moderate man can make his own.[5]

Here a beautiful place evokes a sense of gratitude and joy in the beholder; prayer is the natural response for Socrates. He calls upon the god of nature, Pan, the singing, sensuous, smiling Nourisher, and all other unknown, unnamed dieties, that their external beauty, seen in nature, might be internalized by Socrates and all wise men. And as he strives for inner beauty, Socrates prays that the externals, his possessions and his relationship to the community, may be in accord with his inner beauty and wisdom; that is, moderate, not ostentatious, not superficial, not excessive. In other words, gold, public acclaim, and power should never be primary or in excess for the wise man. The public status of men should be a modest reflection of the riches of the inner man, just the opposite of the hollowness of some public figures. The good citizen must first be a good man.

When he knows himself, and especially his own limitations, then he will be able to serve well the community in which he lives.

Such public responsibility is presupposed in the prayer of an Athenian in the *Laws:*

> Let us call upon God for his assistance towards the organization of the city. May he hear us, and hearing, come to us in mercy and loving-kindness, ready to join in ordering the city and its laws.[6]

This prayer is a fine example of the communal nature of Greek religion: it begins "Let us pray," not "I feel like praying." Indeed the technical term for corporate worship is liturgy, coming from the Greek word for a public activity or work done for the community; only later on in its linguistic development did *leitourgia* come to mean specifically religious action, that is, corporate worship. It is presupposed that God wills and inspires men to order well their public life, and that public prayer is an appropriate preparation for forging public policy and renewing the life of the community.

Prayer in Greek thought is, of course, not limited to public occasions, but is understood to be appropriate and indeed required for all undertakings, whether seemingly trivial or apparently very profound. So, for example, Timaeus says:

> All who have even a small share of sense, Socrates, always call upon God, I think, at the start of any enterprise small or great. Now we are intending to discuss the universe and the question how it has been created or possibly is not a work of creation. Unless we are quite mad, we must

call upon both gods and goddesses and pray that we may
speak what is after their mind, and correspondingly what
is after our own.[7]

Finally, there is a fine conversation about prayer, which
sums up the theme of individual integrity with communal
responsibililty we have seen both in the myth of the cave
and in some of the prayers of Socrates and his friends. In
the *Laws* we have this remarkable conversation about our
intentions in prayer:

> *An Athenian:* Come now, have we shown that there is one
> common desire shared by every man?
> *Megillus:* What desire?
> *Athenian:* That all created things should be according to
> the promptings of his own soul, or if not all things, at
> any rate all that concerns human life.
> *Megillus:* Well?
> *Athenian:* Why then, if that is what we all always want,
> whether children or grown-ups, we should necessarily
> pray for it continually, should we not?
> *Megillus:* Of course.
> *Athenian:* And further, I suppose we should unite with
> our friends in praying for this, which they are praying
> for for themselves.
> *Megillus:* Well?
> *Athenian:* A son is dear to his father, the boy to the man.
> *Megillus:* Of course.
> *Athenian:* But further, when the boy prays that something
> may happen to him, on many occasions the father
> would pray the gods that it may not happen according
> to his son's prayers at all.
> *Megillus:* You mean when the son prays while he is still
> young and foolish.
> *Athenian:* And also when the father, being old, or rather

> all too young, and knowing nothing of what is seemly or right, prays very vehemently and in a passion akin to that of Theseus against his hapless son, the dying Hippolytus—but the boy knows better. Think you that the boy will join in his father's prayers?
>
> *Megillus:* I see what you mean. You mean, I believe, that what is to be prayed and pressed for is not that everything should follow one's desire, but rather that one's desire should follow one's reason. To possess wisdom is what a whole community and every one of us must pray for and endeavor to promote.
>
> *Athenian:* Yes.[8]

Yes indeed! Or as the speakers of Aramaic would have said at this time, "Amen." Here in a brief conversation is the very heart of classical Greek theology and the prayer and worship it presupposes: every human being has one desire in common, that the whole world should be like his own soul; that is, that all things should be made and operate in his own image and reflect his individual desires. Yet when these individualists come together in common life and worship, their individualism inevitably leads to conflicting prayers; for example, the immature boy praying for something foolish that his wise father would not want for him, and much more tragically, the case of the passionate curses of Theseus against his innocent son Hippolytus. So right prayer must not be individualistic and self-centered, trying, as it were, to make the world in one's own image. On the contrary, true prayer must be in accord with one's reason, which is a rationality shared by all human beings. Self-centered desire must give way to our common humanity and the wisdom that transcends us all. It is in the play *Hippolytus* that this theme is most brilliantly portrayed.

THE CURSE AT THE SEASHORE

In the last conversation we have just read from Plato's dialogue, the *Laws,* we noted a reference to King Theseus and "his hapless son, the dying Hippolytus"; their story is told by the dramatist Euripides in his tragedy the *Hippolytus.* The play deals with the conflict between the chaste Hippolytus, devoted to the goddess Artemis and enraptured by love of nature and the hunt, and his stepmother, Phaedra, who is blindly in love with him. When Hippolytus learns from Phaedra's old nurse of his stepmother's passion for him, he is appalled and enraged:

> O Mother Earth! O Sun and open sky! What words I have heard from this accursed tongue! . . . Now at home the mistress plots the mischief, and the maid carries it abroad. So you, vile woman, came here to me to bargain and to traffic in the sanctity of my father's marriage bed. I'll go to a running stream and pour its waters into my ear to purge away the filth. Shall I who cannot even hear such impurity, and feel myself untouched, . . . shall I turn sinner? Woman, know this. It is my piety saves you. Had you not caught me off my guard and bound my lips with an oath, by heaven I would not refrain from telling this to my father. Now I will go and leave this house until Theseus returns from his foreign wanderings. And I'll be silent. But I'll watch you close. I'll walk with my father step by step and see how you look at him, . . . you and your mistress both. I have tasted of the daring of your infamy. I'll know it for the future. Curses on you![9]

Hippolytus is doubly tested, but he only recognizes one side of his crisis. On the natural level, his loyalty to his father, Theseus, is tempted by Theseus' false wife, Phaedra, who would betray her husband and seduce her stepson, if she could. Hippolytus curses this betrayal and strongly asserts his individualism and independence of others; he knows he is pure and that is all that matters. But on the supernatural level, which he does not recognize, his total devotion to the goddess Artemis evokes the enmity of Aphrodite, the goddess of love.[10] It is this one-sided piety which occasions Hippolytus' destruction. He said self-righteously to the old nurse: "My piety saves you." Having made an oath not to tell of what he came to learn, Hippolytus does not speak the whole truth to his father, even when Theseus falsely thinks that his son has committed adultery with his wife. So the excessive piety of Hippolytus, as well as the superficial knowledge and prejudice of his father, bring about the curse that kills an innocent victim.

When Theseus returned home, he found the dead body of his wife, who had taken her own life, and in her hand a tablet, on which she had falsely accused his son. As he begins to read his wife's last message, Theseus asks:

What can she wish to tell me of news?
Have you written begging me to care
for our children or, in entreaty,
about another woman? Sad one, rest confident.
There is no woman in the world who shall come to
    this house
and sleep by my side.
Look, the familiar signet ring,
hers who was once my wife! . . .
    (The Chorus of women speak singly:)
Surely some God
brings sorrow upon sorrow in succession. . . .
The house of our lords is destroyed: it is no more. . . .
God, if it so may be, hear my prayer.

18

Do not destroy this house utterly. I am a prophet:
I can see the omen of coming trouble.
What is it? Tell us if we may share the story.
  (Theseus:)
It cries aloud, this tablet, cries aloud,
and Death is its song! . . .
I shall no longer hold this secret prisoner
in the gates of my mouth. It is horrible,
yet I will speak.
Citizens,
Hippolytus has dared to rape my wife.
He has dishonored God's holy sunlight.
  (He turns in the direction of the sea.)
Father Poseidon, once you gave to me
three curses. . . . Now with one of these, I pray,
kill my son. Suffer him not to escape,
this very day, if you have promised truly.[11]

Theseus will not listen to his son's protestations of innocence. Both father and son are adamant in their individualism and inflexible in their understanding of piety and justice. Hippolytus refuses to modify his rash oath to the old nurse to keep her secret, even when a greater good would have been served by breaking that oath and speaking the full truth to his father. His legalistic piety saved the memory of his stepmother for a while, but at the cost of his own life. Likewise Theseus' outraged sense of justice and personal injury blinded him to all the evidence surrounding his wife's death. Without carefully weighing all the facts, and without heeding the full consequences, he rashly cursed and condemned his son.

The play ends with the dying Hippolytus being brought

back by his comrades from the seashore where the god Poseidon raised up a monstrous savage bull which panicked the horses Hippolytus was driving; they bolted and dragged his body across the sand and rocks. In the epilogue of the play, the goddess Artemis appears to Theseus and reveals the truth:

> Miserable man, what joy have you in this?
> you have murdered a son, you have broken nature's
>   laws.
> Dark indeed was the conclusion
> you drew from your wife's lying accusations,
> but plain for all to see is the destruction
> to which they led you.
> There is a hell beneath the earth: haste to it,
> and hide your head there! . . .
> Hear me tell you, Theseus, how these things came
>   to pass.
> I shall not better them, but I will give you pain.
> I have come here for this—to show you that
>   your son's heart
> was always just, so just that for his good name
> he endured to die. I will show you, too,
> the frenzied love that seized your wife. . . .
> But he, just man, did not fall in with her
> counsels, and even when reviled by you
> refused to break the oath he had pledged.
> Such was his piety. But your wife fearing
> lest she be proved the sinner wrote a letter,
> a letter full of lies; and so she killed
> your son by treachery; but she convinced you.[12]

The last words of the dying Hippolytus to his grieving father are of forgiveness; in their closing conversation with each other they say:

[*Hipp.*] Father, lay hold on me and lift me up.
    [*Thes.*] Alas, what are you doing to me, my son?
I am dying. I can see the gates of death.
    And so you leave me, my hands stained with murder.
No, for I free you from all guilt in this.
    You will acquit me of blood guiltiness?
So help me Artemis. . . .
    Woe for your goodness, piety and virtue.
Farewell to you, too, father, a long farewell!
    Dear son, bear up. Do not forsake me.
This is the end of what I have to bear.
I'm gone. Cover my face up quickly.[13]

In summary, the play *Hippolytus* is tragic because neither the father, Theseus, nor the son, Hippolytus, really know themselves in the way Socrates recognized his ignorance and dependence upon the higher world of reason for guidance in this world of conflict and confusion. Theseus let his passions run away with him after hastily jumping to the wrong conclusion as to the cause of his wife's death. Hippolytus too was a victim of his feelings of excessive devotion to Artemis at the expense of loyalty to others. In the life and teaching of Socrates we see how individual vocation is balanced by responsibility for the community. When this sense of corporate fellowship is missing, as in the *Hippolytus,* we can see how individualism and emotionalism may lead to passionate curses and tragic results.

Mountain and Wilderness

THEMES FOR REFLECTION AND DISCUSSION

1. What role does individualism play in worship today? Is prayer, for example, primarily what I do and feel, or what we do in relationship to God? Some persons have felt that their communion with God was so intimate and intensely personal that they might only distort or corrupt it if they spoke very much to others about their experiences and growth in prayer. An illustration of this attitude may be found in the sublime hymn published about 1367 by Bianco da Siena, who prayed, "Come down, O Love divine, Seek thou this soul of mine, . . ." ending with the lines: "And so the yearning strong, With which the soul will long, Shall far out-pass the power of human telling; For none can guess its grace, Till he become the place Wherein the Holy Spirit makes his dwelling."[14] Bianco seems to be saying that our human telling power is far surpassed by the yearning of each individual believer seeking to become a temple for God's Holy Spirit. Words simply cannot communicate the depths of our religious ardor.

On the other hand, the Moravian newspaper editor, James Montgomery, could write in 1818 a poem with a whole series of definitions describing prayer: "Prayer is the soul's sincere desire, Unuttered or expressed, . . . a hidden fire . . . in the breast, . . . the burden of a sigh, . . . the simplest form of speech, . . . the Christian's vital breath, . . ."[15] His fine hymn on prayer ends with a prayer: "O thou by whom we come to God, The Life, the Truth, the Way, The path of prayer thyself hast trod: Lord, teach us how to pray." That is, prayer for James Montgomery seems to be an art, whose style and content we may discuss with others for our mutual benefit. Where do you find yourself in relationship to these two understandings of how much we can talk to each other about prayer? Are they in conflict?

2. Is a curse ever appropriate in prayer? May a Christian, for example, pray, or say in great earnestness, "God, damn Adolf Hitler!" or "God, crush that tyrant of Uganda!" If not, how do you respond in prayer and worship to persons obviously evil and hateful to you? Or do you simply ignore them in your prayers? Could you pray for them? How?

3. The role of reason is of great importance in Greek civilization. It is likely that Paul was struggling with the relationship between emotions and reason when he wrote to the Corinthians that all things in their worship should be done decently and in order (1 Cor 14:40). We too need to reflect very seriously about the importance of these two aspects of worship, and determine what is an appropriate balance and proportion between the emotional and the rational for fruitful prayer today. Christian hymnody through the centuries has been a valuable means of uniting profound theological thought with deeply moving music. Can you think of other happy unions, where the rational and the emotional have served together well in furthering our worship?

OPTIONAL LENTEN STUDY GUIDE

1. The Collect for the First Sunday in Lent introduces the six Sundays before Easter with these words:

> Almighty God, whose blessed Son was led by the Spirit to be tempted by Satan: Come quickly to help us who are assaulted by many temptations; and, as you know the weaknesses of each of us, let each one find you mighty to save; through Jesus Christ your Son our Lord, who lives

23

and reigns with you and the Holy Spirit, one God, now and for ever.[16]

Reference is made here to Jesus' being tempted by Satan, a highly individualistic and personal experience. Yet note how it is assumed that from that solitary experience in the wilderness of temptation comes a concern for all of us who are also assaulted by many temptations. Like Plato's philosopher, after the individual has been struggling alone, he returns to his companions to help them. Or in the unforgettable words of John Donne, Dean of St. Paul's Cathedral, "No man is an *Island,* entire of itself. . . . I am involved in *Mankind. . . .*"

2. Have a look at Psalm 109, noting especially the long curse in verses 6–19. Compare it with what is possibly the earliest missionary hymn in English, "Jesus shall reign where'er the sun Doth his successive journeys run."[17] This fine hymn was written by the Independent minister, Isaac Watts, in 1719. The hymn continues, "To him shall endless prayer be made, . . . Blessings abound where'er he reigns; . . ." Do you find a connection between a curse and a blessing? Does a blessing presuppose a curse, just as salvation requires sin, and wholeness responds to brokenness?

3. It is fascinating to compare two hymns often sung during Lent.[18] The first is by the Baptist minister Cornelius Elven, who wrote in 1852, "With broken heart and contrite sigh, A trembling sinner, Lord, I cry." The second is an ancient Latin hymn, stemming from the middle ages: "The glory of these forty days We celebrate with songs of praise; For Christ, by whom all things were made, Himself has fasted and has prayed." The first hymn repeats the personal pronoun "I" six times, and uses "me" or "my" nine

times; the second hymn uses "we," "us," or "our" only four times. The first hymn is emotional and subjective; the second hymn is more rationalistic and objective in its recitation and celebration of the great saints of prayer in past history. Which approach do you prefer? Why?

II

ABRAHAM AND MOSES
IN THE WORSHIP OF ISRAEL

ABRAHAM'S CALL FROM THE PLAIN

What has Athens to do with Jerusalem?[1] For the early Christian, Tertullian, the answer was easy: nothing at all. He thought that the revelation of the Bible was unique and the wisdom of the nonbiblical world was to be ignored, if not despised. Tertullian, however, represents a minority opinion. Most Christians have seen in the great achievements of culture and piety in other civilizations a preparation for, or a first step toward, the more complete inspiration that came to Israel and was to reach its fulfillment in Jesus. For example, we have already seen how Socrates heard of the word from the temple at Delphi about himself and how it marked the beginning of his mission and message for others that they should examine their lives with new depth and seriousness. "A word from on high" is also an appropriate starting point for consideration of worship and prayer in the Old Testament.[2]

Abraham is the first historical person in the Bible of

whom much is known. Like a founding father of the Jewish nation, Abraham appears early in the Old Testament, a man called from on high by God to become a pioneer in establishing a great people, united by their worship of the Lord, and to be a missionary, whose message would be a blessing for many others. Abraham's call is found in Genesis 12:1–4:

> Now the Lord said to Abram, "Go from your country and your kindred and your father's house to the land that I will show you. And I will make of you a great nation, and I will bless you, and make your name great, so that you will be a blessing. I will bless those who bless you, and him who curses you I will curse; and by you all the families of the earth shall bless themselves." So Abram went, as the Lord had told him. . . . Abram was seventy-five years old when he departed from Haran.

Abraham obeyed the Lord's call.[3] He left his ancestral home in the plains of Mesopotamia with its many gods and ancient Chaldean culture. At the advanced age of seventy-five he began a new life of pilgrimage, exploration, and testing. Like Socrates in the Greek tradition, Abraham felt close to the God who inspired him and guided him day by day in personal and intimate fellowship. Indeed later tradition in the Bible called Abraham God's friend(Is 41:8). The many adventures Abraham experienced in his response to God's call, even the times of most severe testing, are recognized as blessings, occasions for personal growth and greater responsiveness to the will of the Lord.

Abraham, like his contemporaries, worshiped God with animal sacrifices, the widespread custom of his time, as a way of expressing devotion to God and faithfulness to the covenant made with him. Valuable though the gift of a living creature was, the gift of one's mind was more precious, and the struggle to understand the nature and will of God was seen to be more valuable as an expression of worship. A famous example of this growing depth of worship is found in Genesis 18:22–26 where Abraham's concern for justice and his intercession for the people of Sodom is remembered:

> Abraham still stood before the Lord. Then Abraham drew near, and said, "Wilt thou indeed destroy the righteous with the wicked? Suppose there are fifty righteous within the city; wilt thou then destroy the place and not spare it for the fifty righteous who are in it? Far be it from thee to do such a thing, to slay the righteous with the wicked, so that the righteous fare as the wicked! Far be that from thee! Shall not the Judge of all the earth do right?" And the Lord said, "If I find at Sodom fifty righteous in the city, I will spare the whole place for their sake."

Fifty, forty-five, forty, thirty, twenty, or even ten righteous persons in the midst of an evil city are sufficient to preserve life there. Gerhard Von Rad analyzes this important story with great insight:

> The reader may want to keep in mind the place where [the conversation] occurred, namely, on one of the heights east of Hebron in view of the sinful city lying at a distance in the valley. . . . Basically, Abraham is wrestling, as his appeal to the righteous Judge of the world clearly shows, with a new interpretation of the concept "the righteousness of God. . . ." Does Yahweh's "righteousness" with regard to Sodom not consist precisely in the fact that he will forgive the city for the sake of these innocent ones? . . . It was not, of course, the primary

intention of the text to extol Abraham as the paradig-
matic, prophetic intercessor. But the narrator would
scarcely feel himself badly misunderstood if we were to
read his text from the viewpoint of intercession and its
power.[4]

In Abraham we find new appreciation of what worship
really means. Abraham's vision of God called him away
from the past polytheism of his forefathers to the worship
of the one righteous God, to a new life in a new land, and
to a new seriousness about God, his nature, and his will for
us. Abraham is remarkable in his old age. He did not look
back with nostalgia or bitterness, nor treat his senior years
as a time of withdrawal and increasing passivity. At age
seventy-five he found a concrete goal to be realized in the
future, a mission to found and cultivate a new community,
righteous and outgoing, whose goodness would overflow
and enrich others, both good and bad. Abraham was not
cantankerous. For example, he did not seize the quick solu-
tion for immoral and deviant neighbors, which was to let
them be destroyed and forgotten. Like Socrates, Abraham
saw that evil is no final threat to goodness, even though it
may appear to triumph over the good. Called up higher,
from the lowlands of the many gods of Mesopotamia to the
heights of his new homeland, Abraham could see more
clearly from that inspiration point that God is both one and
righteous: all good actions must succeed because their mo-
tivation and ultimate strength come from the righteous
God himself. A good man, therefore, need not act fearfully
as though evil were ultimately victorious. God's righteousness abides—that is sufficient security for the man of faith.

In a later age, we read in Nehemiah 9:6–8, Ezra could

look back in a prayer of thanksgiving for the type of commitment and confidence Abraham represented:

> Thou art the Lord, thou alone; thou hast made heaven, the heaven of heavens, with all their host, the earth and all that is on it, the seas and all that is in them; and thou preservest all of them; and the host of heaven worships thee. Thou art the Lord, the God who didst choose Abram and bring him forth out of Ur of the Chaldeans and give him the name Abraham; and thou didst find his heart faithful before thee, and didst make with him the covenant to give to his descendants the land of the Canaanite, the Hittite, the Amorite, the Perizzite, the Jebusite, and the Girgashite; and thou hast fulfilled thy promise, for thou art righteous.

The supreme example of worship in the life of Abraham comes in Genesis 22:2,6–14, where Abraham is called upon to sacrifice his son and heir, Isaac—the ultimate test of his faith in God:

> "Take your son, your only son Isaac, whom you love, and go to the land of Moriah, and offer him there as a burnt offering upon one of the mountains of which I shall tell you. . . ." And Abraham took the wood of the burnt offering, and laid it on Isaac his son; and he took in his hand the fire and the knife. So they went both of them together. And Isaac said to his father Abraham, "My father!" And he said, "Here am I, my son." He said, "Behold, the fire and the wood; but where is the lamb for a burnt offering?" Abraham said, "God will provide himself the lamb for a burnt offering, my son." So they went both of them together. When they came to the place of which God had told him, Abraham built an altar there, and laid the wood in order, and bound Isaac his son, and

laid him on the altar, upon the wood. Then Abraham put forth his hand, and took the knife to slay his son. But the angel of the Lord called to him from heaven, and said, "Abraham, Abraham!" And he said, "Here am I." He said, "Do not lay your hand on the lad or do anything to him; for now I know that you fear God, seeing you have not withheld your son, your only son, from me." And Abraham lifted up his eyes and looked, and behold, behind him was a ram, caught in a thicket by his horns; and Abraham went and took the ram, and offered it up as a burnt offering instead of his son. So Abraham called the name of that place The Lord will provide; as it is said to this day, "On the mount of the Lord it shall be provided."[5]

There are a number of reasons for the memory of this great story never having faded or disappeared in the many centuries from the time of Abraham, perhaps 1700 B.C., to the present. First of all, the practice of human sacrifice in general, and child sacrifice especially, was widespread in the ancient world.[6] It was believed that for real success a high price had to be paid to the gods. Here, however, the people of God learned from their founding father that the Lord does not want that kind of worship. Indeed, the Lord provides an animal to substitute in Isaac's place, just as in the New Testament, God's own Son would serve as a sacrifice for many, for a fallen humanity (Mk 10:45; 14:24). The costliness of Abraham's sacrifice, even if it be one's only son, is less important than the quality of worship offered to God. Even our most precious possession is inadequate to buy God's favor or merit his blessing. What is required is unfailing trust, generous obedience, and a readiness to hear God's voice calling for a change in our earlier understanding of his will for his people.

Thus the second quality of Abraham's faith to be noted is his flexibility. He had made up his mind to do what God called him to do. But even having reached the point of no return, he was still open to new revelation from above and fresh insight into his most appropriate response to God. And so by recognizing that he would be wrong if he went any further with the sacrifice of his son, Abraham achieved a turning point in man's understanding of how God is to be worshiped: on the mount of the Lord God provides his own sacrifice if we can remain sensitive to others and increasingly perceptive of the right action appropriate to each new circumstance of our life.

A third quality which makes this story especially memorable is Abraham's responsiveness to God's voice without delay or elaboration. Part of God's test for Abraham was simply to call his name, "Abraham!" The reply is immediate: "Here am I, use me as you will" is what Abraham seems to say. God is his friend and he speaks to him as man to man. And after hearing the awesome order to take his son and sacrifice him as a burnt offering upon one of the mountains, Abraham said nothing to excuse himself, but moved forward as best he could to do the terrible task put upon him by his God. Though he must have agonized over the demand, he did not vacillate in paralyzed indecision. And in his action, his prompt movement to obey God, he received the final word from on high, a complete revelation which saved both his son and himself. Abraham's physical ascent up the mountain without procrastination moved him forward and upward to a new encounter with his Creator and to a far more adequate understanding of the meaning of worship. As Micah (6:7f.) was to declare perhaps a thousand years after Abraham's great discovery:

"Shall I give my first-born for my transgression,
   the fruit of my body for the sin of my soul?"
He has showed you, O man, what is good;
   and what does the Lord require of you
but to do justice, and to love kindness,
   and to walk humbly with your God?

MOSES AND THE MOUNTAIN OF GOD'S TORAH

If the patriarch Abraham, living in about 1700 B.C., may well be considered the founding father of the Jewish people, Moses, some four hundred years later, is appropriately called the greatest teacher of Israel.[7] Indeed the philosopher Numenius, who lived in the second century after Christ, claimed that Plato was simply "Moses in Attic dress!"[8] Moses is also known as the great lawgiver of the Old Testament. His life shows clearly that the Torah he gave in God's name was not merely a legalistic set of commandments and prohibitions: Torah for Moses meant a whole way of life, an attitude toward others, a manner of praying and worshiping the Lord God of Israel day and night. Far from the Torah being a heavy burden for Moses and his successors as teachers and lawgivers of Israel, the words of Psalm 1:1–3 rang true to their experience:

Blessed is the man who walks not in the
   counsel of the wicked,
nor stands in the way of sinners,
   nor sits in the seat of scoffers;
but his delight is in the law of the Lord,
   and on his law he meditates day and night.
He is like a tree planted by streams of water,
   that yields its fruit in its season,

and its leaf does not wither.
In all that he does, he prospers.

Moses' own life represents the prosperity and fruitfulness of the first man of God's Torah.

"Rags to riches" is one way to describe Moses' change from being an abandoned baby floating in a reed basket to his adoption by Pharaoh's daughter and his prosperity as a young man brought up in the royal household. But Moses soon learned the instability of worldly success after intervening in a dispute between Egyptian taskmaster and Hebrew serf, and having to flee for his life. After wandering in a foreign land, Moses became a shepherd there, and many years later he came one day to a high mountain and saw a marvelous sight: a flaming bush, burning away, yet never consumed or destroyed by the fire. Here, Moses knew, was holy ground, an inspiration point, surely the mountain of God. Here Moses found a God whose presence did not destroy but brought warmth and light. Here was a God who called Moses by name and told him his own personal name, Yahweh, by which he might be called and worshiped. This great encounter is described in Exodus 3:4,7,9f.; 13ff.:

> God called to him out of the bush, "Moses, Moses!" And he said, "Here am I . . ." Then the Lord said, . . . "Behold, the cry of the people of Israel has come to me, and I have seen the oppression with which the Egyptians oppress them. Come, I will send you to Pharaoh that you may bring forth my people, the sons of Israel, out of Egypt. . . ." Then Moses said to God, "If I come to the people of Israel and say to them, 'The God of your fathers has sent me to you,' and they ask me, 'What is his

name?' what shall I say to them?" God said to Moses, "I AM WHO I AM." And he said, "Say this to the people of Israel, 'I AM has sent me to you.' " God also said to Moses, "Say this to the people of Israel, 'The Lord [Yahweh], the God of your fathers, the God of Abraham, the God of Isaac, and the God of Jacob, has sent me to you': this is my name for ever, and thus I am to be remembered throughout all generations. . . ."

In the story of Abraham, God first began to be known as the One God, the God above the many gods of popular worship. Now Abraham's One God revealed himself to Moses as a very personal and approachable being, whose sacred name could be invoked in time of need and in times of prosperity and rejoicing. And like Abraham, Moses realized that encounter with God in meditation and prayer necessarily led to concrete and dramatic action. Thus Moses very soon led his people out of Egyptian slavery into a new life of freedom—and hardship—as they moved forward to the Promised Land, an event remembered as the Exodus and celebrated in Jewish and Christian worship every year as the Passover.

The institution of the Passover is first described in Exodus 12, when the Lord said to Moses:

> Tell all the congregation of Israel that on the tenth day of this month [the month Nisan, that is, March-April] they shall take every man a lamb. . . . And you shall keep it until the fourteenth day of this month, when the whole assembly of the congregation of Israel shall kill their lambs in the evening. Then they shall take some of the blood, and put it on the two doorposts and the lintel of the houses in which they eat them. They shall eat the flesh that night, roasted; with unleavened bread and bit-

ter herbs. . . . And you shall eat it in haste. It is the Lord's passover. For I will pass through the land of Egypt that night, and I will smite all the first-born in the land of Egypt, both man and beast; and on all the gods of Egypt I will execute judgements: I am the Lord. The blood shall be a sign for you, upon the houses where you are; and when I see the blood, I will pass over you, and no plague shall fall upon you to destroy you, when I smite the land of Egypt. . . ." Then Moses called all the elders of Israel, and said to them, . . . "You shall observe this rite as an ordinance for you and for your sons for ever. And when you come to the land which the Lord will give you, as he has promised, you shall keep this service. . . ." And the people bowed their heads and worshiped.[9]

This celebration of the Passover became in the worship of Israel an impressive and unforgettable service of grateful remembrance for God's great deliverance of his people from slavery, a highpoint of Jewish liturgy each year.[10] Later on, after Jerusalem, with its great temple, became the focal point of worship, observance of the Passover was restricted to the holy city, which became a center of pilgrimage.[11] For example, Luke 2:41 records that Jesus' parents went to Jerusalem every year at the feast of the Passover, and Jesus himself celebrated the Passover in Jerusalem.[12] Finally when the temple was destroyed in A.D. 70, the actual Passover ceremony ceased, but its themes of exodus and liberation continued to be commemorated in yearly family seder meals by Jews throughout the world.[13] Thus the Passover seder is for Jewish people today a living link with their roots in the distant past when their forefathers gave thanks as they shared Moses' vision of a Promised Land.

Moses' revolution against his overlords in Egypt was not,

however, a struggle of the Hebrews simply to become politically independent and free to do what they pleased. Moses saw that absolute liberty does not exist; real freedom comes from grateful dependence upon God alone, who created us and sustains us all the days of our life on earth. So after the exodus from slavery in Egypt, Moses proclaimed a new slavery on Mt. Sinai, a willing service to the Lord God who enabled his people to escape from the slavery of men. The new service would be called Torah, glad obedience to God's law, delight in the will of the Lord. And on Sinai God revealed to Moses the backbone of Torah, the Ten Commandments, as well as the many principles and precepts of Torah which came to be codified and handed on as the law of Moses. Thus prayer with and response to a personal God who cares for us and gives us his name led Moses not only to action for freedom (Exodus) but also to obedience for perfect freedom (Torah).

The Jewish creed, found in Deuteronomy 6:4f., proclaims and reaffirms this willing slavery three times a day for the faithful:

> Hear, O Israel: The Lord our God is one Lord; and you shall love the Lord your God with all your heart, and with all your soul, and with all your might.

And the next verses of Deuteronomy (6:6–9) show how important is this creed for the life of Israel:

> And these words which I command you this day shall be upon your heart; and you shall teach them diligently to your children, and shall talk of them when you sit in your house, and when you walk by the way, and when you lie down, and when you rise. And you shall bind them as a

37

> sign upon your hand, and they shall be as frontlets be-
> tween your eyes. And you shall write them on the door-
> posts of your house and on your gates.

As the Book of Common Prayer was to describe this willing
slavery so eloquently centuries later: God truly is

> the author of peace and lover of concord, in knowledge
> of whom standeth our eternal life, whose service is per-
> fect freedom.[14]

Here we find a momentous step forward in depth of
perception and quality of worship. Prayer and communion
with God result in concrete laws of worship, conduct, and
relationships with others. The vertical dimension up to
God can stand only on a horizontal base in community and
outgoingness with other people, who are God's people.
Prayer and fellowship with our personal Creator is recognized to be like an equilateral triangle: the higher and
nearer to God we ascend, the wider, more embracing, more
catholic must be our responsiveness to others in right action and ethical conduct. The Torah of the Lord shows us
that love of neighbor is an essential part of God's service;
in time the teaching of Leviticus 19 (1,15,18) would be
appended to the creed of Deuteronomy (6:4) to clarify and
stress this inseparable unity between love of God and love
of neighbor:

> And the Lord said to Moses, "Say to all the congregation
> of the people of Israel, You shall be holy; for I the Lord
> your God am holy. . . . You shall do no injustice in
> judgment; you shall not be partial to the poor or defer
> to the great, but in righteousness shall you judge your
> neighbor. . . . You shall not take vengeance or bear any

grudge against the sons of your own people, but you shall love your neighbor as yourself: I am the Lord.

As the prophet of Nazareth was to teach later on, there is no other commandment greater than these, or, as Matthew 22:40 records Jesus' words: "On these two commandments depend all the law and the prophets." A Jewish scribe replied to Jesus' understanding of Moses' Torah in Mark 12:32f.:

> You are right, Teacher; you have truly said that [the Lord God of Israel] is one, and there is no other but he; and to love him with all the heart, and with all the understanding, and with all the strength, and to love one's neighbor as oneself, is much more than all whole burnt offerings and sacrifices.

We can appreciate why the author of the Epistle to the Hebrews devoted more than half of his eleventh chapter (8–29), the splendid roll call of faith, to Abraham and Moses. By faith "Abraham obeyed." By faith "they were not afraid." By faith Moses "kept the Passover." By faith "the people crossed the Red Sea as if on dry land."[15]

In summary, Abraham and Moses both introduce the importance of this world and its ongoing history into the realm of worship. Prayer and communion with God led Abraham to move from his homeland to new territory so as to found a new community, whereas Socrates never wanted to travel far from his beloved Athens and his fellow citizens. Abraham looked forward into history and saw the promise of the great nation he would establish, a people who would bring blessing to all the nations of the earth. In contrast, this world and its history, whether past or future, was reckoned by Socrates to be illusion, much less real than the spiritual world above which lay beyond the changes and chances of human history.

Prince Hippolytus too was different from Moses in his response to his communion with God. Worship of the goddess Artemis inspired Hippolytus with no mission to his people nor any sense of historical destiny for them. His religion was purely personal, subjective, an occasion of delight for the individual alone. Moses, on the other hand, had to struggle from the beginning with mission, God-given tasks to lead his people into a great historical destiny in a land of promise, and to teach the nation the laws of the Lord so that every day of their future would bring them closer to the righteous and holy God of Israel.

Thus for both Abraham and Moses, this world and its history is very important as the stage where salvation takes place. And salvation for them is not individualistic: we are called by the God of Israel to be his people, not his individuals. Together in corporate worship and mutual commitment to our God and to each other, we move forward in response to his Torah from on high.

THEMES FOR REFLECTION AND DISCUSSION

1. Abraham and Moses lived in a polytheistic society, yet came to realize that there was only one God who deserved worship and loyalty. Is polytheism, the adoration of many gods, an issue for worshipers today? If so, what are some of the false gods of our society? Francis Bacon, writing in England at the time of the arrival of the Pilgrim Fathers in America, said that there were many idols and false notions which possessed us and dominated our understanding;

these he called Idols of the Tribe, Idols of the Den (our individual prejudices), Idols of the Market Place, and Idols of the Theater. How would you describe and catalogue our idols in contemporary life? Can you clarify the distinction between God, gods, and idols?

2. Abraham and Moses were relatively old when they encountered God and began their arduous travel and struggles. What does the increasingly greater average age of our society imply for worship today? Classical culture generally looked upon aging as a disaster: as Lord Byron recalled, " 'Whom the gods love die young' was said of yore." Certainly Shakespeare in *As You Like It* had hard words to say about our last days on earth: if all the world's a stage, the last scene that ends our strange eventful history "Is second childishness, and mere oblivion, Sans teeth, sans eyes, sans taste, sans everything." Do we have a different understanding of aging today? Does the senior citizen have a particular witness to bear about the meaning of life in general, and the function of prayer in particular, as a quality control for human existence? How do you respond to the aging of others—and yourself?

3. Abraham and Moses both illustrate faith in God and concrete action in the historical development of their people. Is history only "bunk," as Henry Ford said in the witness box? If not, what relevance do past history, future aspirations, and present actions to bring about that future and to fulfill that past have for worship today? Is prayer passive, or is it a springboard for action?

OPTIONAL LENTEN STUDY GUIDE

1. The Collect for the Second Sunday in Lent:

> O God, whose glory it is always to have mercy:
> Be gracious to all who have gone astray from
> your ways, and bring them again with penitent
> hearts and steadfast faith to embrace and
> hold fast the unchangeable truth of your
> Word, Jesus Christ your Son; who with you
> and the Holy Spirit lives and reigns, one God,
> for ever and ever.[16]

Here we pray for God's grace upon people who have gone astray from God's ways. Socrates, too, spoke of life as a journey, for the wise man leading to the Good, the Beautiful, and the True, with only the foolish deviating from that goal. Abraham and Moses were two great examples of men who chose pilgrimage, a long trip toward distant goals as they followed God's ways. It was, however, John Bunyan, the impressive Baptist preacher and remarkable writer of seventeenth-century England, who wrote a work that elaborates this theme of pilgrimage with unforgettable artistry and power, his *Pilgrim's Progress*. Some lines from that work have become a well-known hymn:

> He who would valiant be
> 'Gainst all disaster,
> Let him in constancy
> Follow the Master.

> There's no discouragement
> Shall make him once relent
> His first avowed intent
> To be a pilgrim.[17]

The rest of this great hymn, as well as the splendid chapter in which it appears, entitled "Mr. Valiant-for-Truth," are surely worth reading again as an unfolding expression of the meaning of pilgrimage for Bunyan's time—and ours.

2. But note that persons can miss or detour from the way of the Lord. For example, some have never heard God's name taken seriously and used in love, but only in a curse with rage, or as a swear word, or trivially in meaningless sentimentality. Others detour from God because some people with God's name on their lips are so distasteful in their conduct that they contaminate and deface the beauty and attractiveness of God's ways. Uriah Heep, the pious fraud in Dicken's *David Copperfield,* is a classic example, unfortunately still to be encountered from time to time in religious circles today. What examples could you cite of deviating forces, repellent personal qualities, and other roadblocks which turn people away from God's way, the true way of delight and fulfillment? To what degree is each one of us guilty of blocking others? How do we impede them?

3. The prayer for the second Sunday in Lent speaks of penitence and faith as a way of bringing back to God's way those who have gone astray. Penitence means feeling profoundly sorry for one's sin. Is this sorrow a necessary part of Christian joy? For example, must we experience a Good Friday before we can truly appreciate the joy of Easter?

Mountain and Wilderness

What about tendencies in our society to minimize, masquerade with, or deny outright, the reality of death, the objective quality of evil, the appropriateness at times of guilt? Select a hymn which expresses well the balance between penitence and rejoicing. Why does it succeed? Does it correspond to your own experience?

III

THE PRAYERS
OF DAVID AND SOLOMON

THE PRAYER BOOK OF ISRAEL

The Psalms of David have often been called the prayer book of the Old Testament. A hundred and fifty of them comprise the Psalter, which has been treasured by Jew and Christian alike.[1] Many of these prayers and hymns come from the time of King David himself, a thousand years before Christ, and not a few may come from David's own hand with only minor editing through the centuries.[2] Other psalms, composed later in the ongoing history of the Jewish nation, are nonetheless written in the name of David and in his spirit, intending to extend his understanding of worship to new times and places.

A fresh chapter in the history of Israel's worship is reached when hymns and prayers are written not only for use in a specific situation, perhaps of pressing need, but also at the same time are intended to meet future needs of other people not yet living. By writing down and handing on a collection of psalms, David and his fellow psalmists

underlined the corporate nature of worship in an unforgettable way. They recognized that the delight and inspiration
of one experience of prayer and meditation could be a
springboard for others to enter into that pleasure.

For example, Psalm 84:1–3,9, in the fine modern translation of The Proposed Book of Common Prayer captures
the shared delight that accompanies fellowship and worship by the people of God:

How dear to me is your dwelling, O Lord of hosts!
    My soul has a desire and longing for the
                courts of the Lord;
    my heart and my flesh rejoice in the living God.
The sparrow has found her a house
and the swallow a nest where she may lay her young;
    by the side of your altars, O Lord of hosts,
    my King and my God.
Happy are they who dwell in your house!
    they will always be praising you. . . .
For one day in your courts is better
                than a thousand in my own room,
    and to stand at the threshold of the house of my God
    than to dwell in the tents of the wicked.

Here corporate worship and the prayer of the community come to their finest flower. David was responsible
for the capture of Jerusalem and its establishment as the
capital of his growing kingdom. David also laid the plans
for a glorious house of the Lord, a great temple wherein
God might be worshiped in fitting reverence, splendor,
and solemnity. The daily services of prayer and sacrifice
in the temple were to become the foundation of Jewish
piety for a thousand years, an occasion for refreshing

worship and new inspiration from the living God. The last verse of Psalm 84 expresses with exactness the experience of David and his successors in great moments of prayer:

> O Lord of hosts,
>> happy are they who put their trust in you!

But the psalms also can articulate for the people of God the depths of depression and estrangement. The most memorable expression of feelings of deep alienation is Psalm 22:1–4,10f.:

My God, my God, why have you forsaken me?
   and are so far from my cry
   and from the words of my distress?
O my God, I cry in the daytime, but you do not answer;
   by night as well, but I find no rest.
Yet you are the Holy One,
   enthroned upon the praises of Israel.
Our forefathers put their trust in you;
   they trusted, and you delivered them. . . .
I have been entrusted to you ever since I was born;
   you were my God when I was still in my
      mother's womb.
Be not far from me, for trouble is near,
   and there is none to help.

Certainly David's own life illustrates the reversals, weariness, and sickness which underlie Psalm 22. Although David had won victory over the enemies of his king, his success and popularity soon aroused the envy of King Saul. After several narrow escapes from the death Saul had plotted against him, David had to go into hiding. It was only after the defeat of King Saul at the hands of the Philistines that David was free to give up his life as a refugee. But it was hollow good fortune, for both the King, his persecutor, and Saul's son, Jonathan, his greatest friend, were slain. David's lament over them is one of the oldest and most moving parts of the Bible. It is found in the Second Book of Samuel (1:19f.,23–27):

Thy glory, O Israel, is slain upon thy high places!
   How are the mighty fallen!
Tell it not in Gath,
   publish it not in the streets of Ashkelon;
lest the daughters of the Philistines rejoice,
   lest the daughters of the uncircumcised exult. . . .
Saul and Jonathan, beloved and lovely!
   In life and in death they were not divided;
they were swifter than eagles,
   they were stronger than lions.
Ye daughters of Israel, weep over Saul,
   who clothed you daintily in scarlet,
   who put ornaments of gold upon your apparel.
How are the mighty fallen
   in the midst of the battle!
Jonathan lies slain upon thy high places.
I am distressed for you, my brother Jonathan;
very pleasant have you been to me;
   your love to me was wonderful,
   passing the love of women.
How are the mighty fallen,
   and the weapons of war perished!

The excellence of the Psalms of David is their ability to articulate not only the heights and depths of religious feeling, but also the ups and downs of everyday life. Both the mountaintop experience of delight in the Lord and the valley of the shadow of death are in the prayer book of Israel. David's own life suggests more than once that the two are related: it was in his ability to accept and cope with frustration and defeat that new growth and victory became possible.

Psalm 23 (1–4), the greatest of the psalms attributed to David, is the finest hymn in the Psalter, reflecting David's abiding trust in the Lord, so that even disaster could be an occasion for creativity and forward movement. In the fine translation of the new Prayer Book:

> The Lord is my shepherd;
>   I shall not be in want.
> He makes me lie down in green pastures
>   and leads me beside still waters.
> He revives my soul
>   and guides me along right pathways for his
>   Name's sake.
> Though I walk through the valley of
>   the shadow of death,
> I shall fear no evil;
>   for you are with me;
>   your rod and your staff, they comfort me.

Here the theme of pilgrimage, progress toward the Promised Land, so important for Abraham and Moses, is given a personal interpretation. This psalm of David, the former shepherd boy, compares us to the sheep of God, our Shepherd. If I have David's faith that the Lord is my shepherd, then important implications follow from my belief: God has made a plan for his people and lovingly cares for us; in all the ups and downs of our human existence, the Lord is present, to give us rest and nourishment, refreshment and peace, new strength and guidance as we go through our days on earth. Even death and the fear of annihilation do not destroy or panic me, "for you are with me"—just as the good shepherd guides and comforts his sheep. On the mountain of God's Torah Moses learned the personal name of God, I Am, being itself, awesome and inspiring. But the psalmist has a new name for the old Reality— Shepherd of Israel, kindly, provident, and urging his people forward. For when "I lift up my eyes to the hills," wondering in hope and fear "from where is my help to come?" the psalmist reminds us that "my help comes from the Lord, the maker of heaven and earth." We read in Psalm 121:1ff.,5,7:

He will not let your foot be moved
    and he who watches over you will not fall asleep. . . .
The Lord himself watches over you;
    the Lord is your shade at your right hand. . . .
The Lord shall preserve you from all evil;
    it is he who shall keep you safe.

There is another part of Moses' understanding of worship that is brought up to date and clarified in the Psalms —delight in the Torah. Psalm 1 was probably selected to be an introduction to the entire Psalter. It serves as a bridge between Moses the lawgiver and David's son, King Solomon, who built the Temple where the Psalms of David were sung and the Torah of Moses was expounded. This prelude to the hundred and forty-nine other psalms begins, in the fine new translation:

> Happy are they who have not walked in
>   the counsel of the wicked,
>   nor lingered in the way of sinners,
>   nor sat in the seats of the scornful!
> Their delight is in the law of the Lord,
>   and they meditate on his law day and night.
> They are like trees planted by streams of water,
> bearing fruit in due season, with leaves
>   that do not wither;
>   everything they do shall prosper.[3]

The songs and prayers of the Psalter, along with the laws and traditions of Israel, are both ingredients for the worship of the Old Testament, the two sides of the one coin —prayer. Offerings and sacrifice in the temple, for example, were not to be separated from obedience to the Ten Commandments: attention to both was required if worship of God was to be real. Personal feelings of joy or despondency, exaltation or gloom, were not to be encapsulated in the individual and his own private piety. He was always a member of the people of God, part of the community of Torah; he was responsible for his relationships to others, accountable for his actions and what bearing his own conduct had on others. As the temple of Solomon became a concrete place where prayer and Torah were united, so too the people of God were increasingly reminded by the prophets of Israel that integrity and mercy—concrete public actions—are the only test we have for sincerity and authenticity in our worship.

KING SOLOMON AND THE WISDOM FROM ON HIGH

The wisdom of Solomon has become proverbial.[4] For example, it is recounted in the delightful story of the visit of the Queen of Sheba in 1 Kings 10:3–9:

> Solomon answered all her questions; there was nothing hidden from the king which he could not explain to her. And when the queen of Sheba had seen all the wisdom of Solomon, the house that he had built, the food of his table, the seating of his officials, and the attendance of his servants, their clothing, his cupbearers, and his burnt offerings which he offered at the house of the Lord, there was no more spirit in her. And she said to the king, "The report was true which I heard in my own land of your affairs and of your wisdom, but I did not believe the reports until I came and my own eyes had seen it; and, behold, the half was not told me; your wisdom and prosperity surpass the report which I heard. Happy are your wives! Happy are these your servants, who continually stand before you and hear your wisdom! Blessed be the Lord your God, who has delighted in you and set you on the throne of Israel!"

The Queen of Sheba's response to Solomon's wisdom was appropriate: she blessed the Lord. For early in Solomon's reign he had a dream in which he prayed for an understanding mind to govern the people of God, and for the wisdom to discern between good and evil. The rest of the vision is described in the third chapter of 1 Kings (verses 10–15):

> It pleased the Lord that Solomon had asked this. And God said to him, "Because you have asked this, and have not asked for yourself long life or riches or the life of

your enemies, but have asked for yourself understanding to discern what is right, behold, I now do according to your word. Behold, I give you a wise and discerning mind, so that none like you has been before you and none like you shall arise after you. I give you also what you have not asked, both riches and honor, so that no other king shall compare with you, all your days. And if you will walk in my ways, keeping my statutes and my commandments, as your father David walked, then I will lengthen your days." And Solomon awoke, and behold, it was a dream.

The king of Israel had to embody many qualities of leadership as chief administrator, judge and lawgiver, commander-in-chief in battle, promotor of the economic welfare and the commonweal of his people. In short, he was very much the head of the state. Wisdom was naturally considered preeminently important for a king, and his wisdom had to be practical, a down-to-earth knowledge of men and affairs. Yet this concrete, day-to-day *savoir faire* was by no means in conflict with religious knowledge, as though involvement in mundane problems of government and civic responsibilities precluded knowledge of and communion with the God of Israel. No, just as we have seen that both psalmody and Torah were integral to the worship in Solomon's temple, so for Solomon himself the fear of the Lord was the beginning of his wisdom.

This understanding of wisdom, as grounded in fear and in reverence for the Lord, is the theme of Psalm 111 and Job 28; and it underlies much of the first nine chapters of the Proverbs of Solomon. A fine illustration of this religious and prayerful foundation for practical wisdom is found in Proverbs 2:1,5–15:

My son, if you receive my words and
    treasure up my commandments with you, . . .
then you will understand the fear of the Lord
    and find the knowledge of God.
For the Lord gives wisdom;
    from his mouth come knowledge and understanding;
he stores up sound wisdom for the upright;
    he is a shield to those who walk in integrity,
guarding the paths of justice
    and preserving the way of his saints.
Then you will understand righteousness and justice
    and equity, every good path;
for wisdom will come into your heart,
    and knowledge will be pleasant to your soul;
discretion will watch over you;
    understanding will guard you;
delivering you from the way of evil,
    from men of perverted speech,
who forsake the paths of uprightness
    to walk in the ways of darkness,
who rejoice in doing evil
    and delight in the perverseness of evil;
men whose paths are crooked
    and who are devious in their ways.

This passage shows belief in divine-human collaboration,
real fellowship, and "teamwork" between the Creator and
wise persons who seek to be creative and share in the con-
structive and onward-moving progress of creation toward
its God-given goals. The Lord bestows wisdom and the
wise man searches for it as for hidden treasure waiting to
be found. To treasure the law of the Lord is the way to find
more wisdom; to practice wisdom by upright action brings

one closer to God, the source of all wisdom. Thus we read in Proverbs 15:8,29:

> The sacrifice of the wicked is an abomination to the Lord, but the prayer of the upright is his delight. . . . The Lord is far from the wicked, but he hears the prayer of the righteous.

while on the other side of the coin, in Proverbs 28:9, we read that:

> If one turns away his ear from hearing the law, even his prayer is an abomination.

So here we find a new synthesis in worship, illustrated by wise King Solomon and the proverbs that bear his name. To worship God aright requires not only the faithful obedience of Abraham, the right conduct of Moses, and the hopefulness of David, but also intelligence. Solomon represents the cognitive and pragmatic side of worship, that indispensable part of authentic prayer which moves us to accomplish some concrete action or change. In the case of the wise man, the action will be appropriate, the change will be for the better, whereas the deeds of a fool are often folly and his worship far short of what his Creator intends. Thus in the proverbs of Solomon our individual responsibility is strongly stressed, and the serious task of clear thinking, careful reflection, and sensitive evaluation is laid upon every sincere person of prayer. Good intentions in meditation are not enough to validate our piety. Our prayers run the risk of being illegitimate or merely trivial unless they flow from fear of the Lord, the beginning of wisdom, and the daily effort to understand God's will and to apply it with intelligence to all the varied actions and responsibilities we have.[5]

The important role assigned to wisdom in the life of the people of God brings about an increasingly valuable new insight into the nature of God and how we ought to pray. Wisdom is more and more understood as feminine. For example, wisdom is often personified as a prophetess, as in Proverbs 1:20ff.:

> Wisdom cries aloud in the street;
> in the markets she raises her voice;
> on the top of the walls she cries out;
> at the entrance of the city gates she speaks:
> "How long, O simple ones, will you love being simple? . . ."

And in Proverbs 8:1–5 we are told:

> Does not wisdom call,
> Does not understanding raise her voice?
> On the heights beside the way,
> in the paths she takes her stand;
> beside the gates in front of the town,
> at the entrance of the portals she cries aloud:
> "To you, O men, I call,
> and my cry is to the sons of men.
> O simple ones, learn prudence;
> O foolish men, pay attention. . . ."

She appears in Proverbs 9:1–6 as a kind lady, calling those in need to the riches of her table:

Wisdom has built her house,
   she has set up her seven pillars.
She has slaughtered her beasts, she has
    mixed her wine,
   she has also set her table.
She has sent out her maids to call
   from the highest places in the town,
"Whoever is simple, let him turn in here!"
   To him who is without sense she says,
"Come, eat of my bread
   and drink of the wine I have mixed,
Leave simpleness, and live,
   and walk in the way of insight."

Here, coming into the strongly masculine and patriarchal world of Abraham and Moses, is an admiration for wisdom and a remarkable recognition of the maternal and feminine qualities of God. The term wisdom is feminine in grammatical gender and in the connotations of the word in Hebrew and Greek. While God is most frequently known as king of Israel, mighty warrior, and merciful judge, he *(he!)* is also womanlike in his (her) creativity and fecundity, his (her) sublime wisdom and practical knowledge of domestic science and home economics in the running of the universe! It is difficult in English to capture the nuances of the Hebrew word *chokmah,* the feminine wisdom of God. But *wisdom* does remind the Hebrews that God is not merely another male being, however highly exalted, but rather the Supreme Being who embraces both masculinity and femininity in creative and fructiferous perfection.

A further recognition of the importance of wisdom is found in the Wisdom of Solomon, which was composed just about the time of Christ, and forms part of the Apocrypha, a group of writings coming between the Old Testament and the New Testament Scriptures. In chapter seven of this attractive work, which praises wisdom and the blessings that come from her to the wise and righteous upon earth, wisdom herself is personified as the "fashioner of all things" (verse 22), "she is a breath of the power of God" (verse 25), and a "spotless mirror of the working of God" (verse 26); "in every generation she passes into holy souls and makes them friends of God, and prophets" (verse 27). In chapter eight, Solomon tells of his love affair with wisdom (verses 2,4,8f.,16,21):

I loved her and sought her from my youth,
and I desired to take her for my bride,
and I became enamored of her beauty. . . .
For she is an initiate in the knowledge of God,
and an associate in his works. . . .
And if any one longs for wide experience,
she knows the things of old, and infers the
    things to come;
she understands turns of speech
    and the solutions of riddles;
she has foreknowledge of signs and wonders
and of the outcome of seasons and times.
Therefore I determined to take her to live with me,
knowing that she would give me good counsel
and encouragement in cares and grief. . . .
When I enter my house, I shall find rest with her,
for companionship with her has no bitterness,
and life with her has no pain, but gladness and joy. . . .
But I perceived that I would not possess wisdom
    unless God gave her to me—

and it was a mark of insight to know whose
   gift she was—
so I appealed to the Lord and besought him, . . .

And in chapter nine we have an exquisite presentation of
how Solomon might have prayed to God (verses 1f.,8ff.,
17):

O God of my fathers and Lord of mercy,
who hast made all things by thy word,
and by thy wisdom hast formed man, . . .
give me the wisdom that sits by thy throne,
and do not reject me from among thy servants. . . .
Thou hast given command to build
   a temple on thy holy mountain,
and an altar in the city of thy habitation,
a copy of the holy tent which thou didst
   prepare from the beginning.
With thee is wisdom, who knows thy works
and was present when thou didst make the world,
and who understands what is pleasing in thy sight
and what is right according to thy commandments.
Send her forth from the holy heavens,
and from the throne of thy glory send her,
that she may be with me and toil,
and that I may learn what is pleasing to thee. . . .
Who has learned thy counsel, unless thou hast
   given wisdom
and sent thy holy Spirit from on high?

This last passage is particularly fascinating because not
only is it an impressive prayer for wisdom but we find in it
that God's wisdom is also called God's holy Spirit. Thus the

old ideas of who God is give way to new richness and profundity. The Creator is from certain standpoints masculine, but from other points of view feminine in quality and style of revelation. God is the source of all goodness and beauty, embracing both what we call masculine and what is feminine. Now, increasingly, God is recognized as outgoing, bestowing wisdom on all who seek her with sincerity and diligence, so that they may do God's will with intelligence and efficiency. God is above and beyond our usual models of power and grandeur, sending with love his Spirit upon all of us who would receive her for guidance, inspiration, and companionship.[6]

In summary, father and son, David and Solomon, represent a movement toward universalizing the worship of the God of Abraham and Moses. With David prayer and meditation take on a literary expression, and the psalms which bear his name are the sublime monument to his effort to worship the Lord with beauty, style, and unforgettable language. By writing down his thoughts and feelings, polishing his words, and perfecting his sentence structure and the logic of his art, David shared with mankind the inspiration he had from on high. Likewise in Solomon we find a universalizing tendency, both in his construction of a great temple where many people from even distant places could come together for worship and celebration of the goodness of the Lord, and above all in his choice of wisdom to be his companion and guide. The God of his fathers Himself became more universal in the theology of Israel. God was recognized to be for all persons, because the Creator was necessarily the source and sustainer of all, embracing all the virtues and delights of creation, whether masculine or feminine. Here is the dawn of that splendid vision which would be vouchsafed later to another wise teacher of Israel: centuries later Paul was to see that "There is neither Jew nor Greek, . . . neither slave nor free, . . . neither male nor female; for you are all one in Christ Jesus. And if you are Christ's, then you are Abraham's offspring, heirs according to promise" (Gal 3:28f.).

THEMES FOR REFLECTION AND DISCUSSION

1. David's lament over the death of his intimate friend Jonathan is world famous. It is remarkable that David included in his sorrow the death of Saul, who had been persecuting David and seeking his life. Would this be an example of what Jesus taught about loving your enemies and praying for those who persecute you (Mt 5:44)? Do you, like David, have enemies today, or at least people whom you genuinely dislike, whom you think may be actively wishing you ill? If not, could it be that your life is so conformist that you are "neither cold nor hot" (Rev 3:15)? If so, what are you doing with your feelings of resentment? Reflect upon the Christian response to confrontation and hostility. How should we deal with feelings of antagonism others may have toward us? How do we cope with our own hostilities and resentments?

2. The role of dreams is considerable in the Bible. It was in a dream that Solomon made his momentous decision to seek Lady Wisdom above all other treasures. Both in the relatively recent study of psychiatry, as well as for a long time in some parts of the Christian Church, great interest has been taken in the role and significance of dreams as a way of articulating truth which cannot be communicated in any other manner. And consider, for example, the great use Martin Luther King, Jr., made of what he called his dreams for his people, his vision for our country. What importance

do you think visions, dreams, and their interpretation should play in your personal life and in the corporate experience and worship of the Church today?

3. The feminine qualities and connotations of God's wisdom have been cited in the women's movement as a theological foundation for many of the current issues women are raising. What particular areas in the present debate do you think can be clarified by the divine femininity? Is the poetical and metaphorical language applied to wisdom a help or a hindrance in understanding such concrete and practical questions as how women should exercise their priesthood in the Church, how sexist language with its built-in prejudices can be removed from preaching and worship, how male arrogance and bigotry should be shown for what it is?

OPTIONAL LENTEN STUDY GUIDE

1. The Collect for the Third Sunday in Lent:

> Almighty God, you know that we have no power in ourselves to help ourselves: Keep us both outwardly in our bodies and inwardly in our souls, that we may be defended from all adversities which may happen to the body, and from all evil thoughts which may assault and hurt the soul; through Jesus Christ our Lord, who lives and reigns with you and the Holy Spirit, one God, for ever and ever.[7]

Note especially the opening words: "we have no power in ourselves to help ourselves." Is that literally true? Do we in fact think that we have no power whatsoever to help ourselves? And if we really don't think this way most of the time, does this mean that the words of the prayer are dead wrong? Or does the prayer perhaps illustrate the possibility of different levels of communicating religious truth, including a nonliteral, poetical, parabolical mode of expression that can reach depths of human experience which cannot be fathomed by ordinary newspaper or telephone-book language? The Psalms of David are a superb example of such metaphorical use of language, as are also the parables of Jesus. It is worth reflecting how many of the prayers in the liturgy of the Church would lose their richness if they were accepted only at face value, prosaically, woodenly, without sensitivity to nuance, metaphor, and liturgical intention.

2. If this Collect were said or sung in corporate worship rather than spoken silently in private prayer, would it take on a fuller dimension, for example, expressing the despair we all feel for our sins and failures to live up to the high destiny our Creator has placed before us? In a profound sense, do we not all need to recognize and lament our impotence, our utter dependence upon God for existence itself? The most sublime and awesome example of sensitive use of prayer comes from Jesus' last words from the cross, as Mark 15:34 records: "And at the ninth hour Jesus cried with a loud voice, *'Eloi, Eloi, lama sabachthani?'* which means, 'My God, my God, why hast thou forsaken me?' " A world of reflection and a lifetime of meditation is needed to begin to understand the literal factualness, the paradoxical truth, and the parabolical profundity of those unforgettable words.

3. *Veni Emmanuel* is one of the loveliest selections of Latin church music we sing during the Advent Season:

> O come, O come, Emmanuel,
> And ransom captive Israel,

That mourns in lonely exile here
Until the Son of God appear.
Rejoice! Rejoice! Emmanuel
Shall come to thee, O Israel!
O come, thou Wisdom from on high,
Who orderest all things mightily;
To us the path of knowledge show,
And teach us in her ways to go.
Refrain
O come, O come, thou Lord of might,
Who to thy tribes on Sinai's height
In ancient times didst give the law,
In cloud, and majesty, and awe. . . .
Refrain
O come, Desire of nations, bind
In one the hearts of all mankind;
Bid thou our sad divisions cease,
And be thyself our King of Peace.
Refrain   Amen.[8]

This hymn incorporates the centuries-old "seven great antiphons," which celebrate the coming of the Messiah. As a daily preparation leading up to Christmas eve, each verse of the hymn would be sung in religious communities on a successive day. It is interesting to note that in verse two the antiphon is addressed to wisdom, and that this particular verse is specifically mentioned in the calendar of the English *Book of Common Prayer* to be sung on December 16th: "O come, thou Wisdom from on high, . . . To us the path of knowledge show, And teach us in her ways to go." It is worth considering whether the antiphon suggests that the "path of knowledge" is primarily to be discovered by us or, on the contrary, is to be revealed to us by the Wisdom from on high. Are we perhaps wrong to imagine that we can simply drive a bulldozer straight through the countryside of human experience, letting our aggressiveness and domineering tendencies impose themselves upon nature? To find the ways of Wisdom may mean that we need to be taught, which might suggest that we must become more attentive, receptive, patient, perceptive, responsive—more feminine.

IV

THE MOUNT
OF TRANSFIGURATION
AND THE WILDERNESS
OF TEMPTATION

LUKE'S PICTURE OF PRAYER IN THE LIFE OF JESUS

Not only does the Gospel of Luke start and conclude with prayer in the temple at Jerusalem, but at all the major turning points in Jesus' career, he is portrayed as first being in prayer and meditation.[1] For example, at Jesus' baptism, Luke 3:21f. reports:

> Now when all the people were baptized, and when Jesus also had been baptized and was praying, the heaven was opened, and the Holy Spirit descended upon him in bodily form, as a dove, and a voice came from heaven, "Thou art my beloved Son; with thee I am well pleased."

It was in this hour of prayer that Jesus for the first time heard himself addressed as the *Son of God.*[2]

Jesus' own self-understanding has been a perennial riddle for his disciples from the beginning to the present. In fact, in Luke 9:18ff., Jesus raised the question himself when he challenged his earliest followers with the problem of the legitimacy and authority of his mission:

> Now it happened that as he was praying alone the disciples were with him; and he asked them, "Who do the people say that I am?" And they answered, "John the Baptist; but others say, Elijah; and others, that one of the old prophets has risen." And he said to them, "But who do you say that I am?" And Peter answered, "The Christ of God."

Like every man of God, Jesus had an ongoing task to clarify for himself and others the validity of his message and to make certain, day by day, that it was in fact, as well as in intention, God's Torah. But unlike others, when Jesus was praying after his baptism, he heard God's voice addressing him, "Thou art my beloved Son."

To be the beloved Son of God was an awesome self-understanding for Jesus to receive at the beginning of his ministry. "Beloved Son" was the description applied to Isaac when his father Abraham had the terrible test put upon them both—the sacrifice of his beloved son to God. When Jesus heard himself called God's beloved Son, and came to realize that such was his vocation and destiny, it was no proud title of self-aggrandizement but a name of sacrifice, full of painful steps leading to a fearful end in total obedience to God's will.

The actual words of Jesus' prayer, when God spoke to him as his beloved Son, are not recorded, but they might have been close to the language of a popular Jewish prayer, known as the *Kaddish,* and containing these petitions:[3]

> Exalted and hallowed be his great name
> > in the world which he created according to
> > > his will.
>
> May he let his kingdom rule
> > in your lifetime and in your days and in
> > > the lifetime of the whole house of Israel,
> > > > speedily and soon.
>
> Praised be his great name from eternity to
> > eternity.
>
> And to this, say: Amen.

If Jesus were praying the *Kaddish* or a prayer in his own words but similar in content, then the meaning of the voice from heaven and Jesus' subsequent mission becomes clearer: God showed that he is not only the heavenly Father of all Israel in general, but that Jesus is particularly and personally close to him as a beloved Son, and as such is called to a sacrifical life and ministry. Jesus' dying words from the cross reveal that supremely personal and intimate relationship: "Father, forgive them; . . . Father, into thy hands I commit my spirit!" (Lk 23:34,46).

A natural response of Jesus to the words he had heard at his baptism from his heavenly Father was for him to teach his disciples to call God "Father," as in the words of the Lord's Prayer, and to devote his life to proclaim and bring about God's reign, his kingdom, that it might increasingly rule in the lives of his people on earth. Thus the ancient prayer known as the *Kaddish* may have been the inspiration or occasion for Jesus to work out the theme of his preaching, that God's kingly rule was already to be found, present and growing in the lives of Jesus and his disciples. In any case, that time of prayer at Jesus' baptism was of fundamental importance for the ministry which followed.

John V. Taylor has a valuable comment upon the uniquely important role prayer played in Jesus' life:

> Considering the richness of Jewish liturgy and family ritual, it is surprising to find a far more frequent use of the various words for prayer in the New Testament than in the Old, and this surely reflects a unique emphasis in the life of Jesus. Patriarchs, prophets and kings had from time to time acted as intercessors for the people, and Moses was the supreme example of this. Yet no figure in the Bible before the appearance of Christ seems to have depended upon the habit of communion with God as Jesus did.[4]

Throughout Jesus' life, prayer and worship were indispensable; they were always the prerequisite of his teaching and the presupposition of his actions.

Jesus went on to choose the Twelve Apostles after remaining in prayer to God all night (Lk 6:12). At crucial times he continued to pray for them and often with them (Lk 22:28–32; 39–46, for example). There is an impressive description by Luke of the inner circle of Jesus' friends, Peter, James, and John, sharing prayer with Jesus on the mount of the transfiguration; Luke 9:28–31 records that:

> He took with him Peter and John and James, and went up on the mountain to pray. And as he was praying, the appearance of his countenance was altered, and his raiment became dazzling white. And behold, two men talked with him, Moses and Elijah, who appeared in glory and spoke of his departure, which he was to accomplish at Jerusalem.

The similarity of Jesus' experience at the transfiguration to Moses' encounter with God, also on a mountaintop as de-

69

scribed in Exodus, is remarkable. Indeed Luke seems to underline it when he specifically mentions the content of Jesus' conversation with Moses and Elijah. They talked about Jesus' departure (in Greek, his *exodus*), which he would accomplish in Jerusalem. Naturally Moses' exodus from slavery in Egypt would come to mind, and it seems clear that Luke wished to draw a parallel to Jesus' own liberation movement, which would begin in Jerusalem and bring religious freedom to the lowly and oppressed throughout the Roman Empire—a story Luke would chronicle and celebrate in the Acts of the Apostles. Here at the transfiguration, Jesus' disciples began to see what was Jesus' own Torah. But only after his exodus, the resurrection, would they fully understand how exceptional was Christ's mission: to fulfill everything written about him in the law of Moses and the prophets and the psalms (Lk 24:44).

For Luke, Jesus embodies the fullness of worship and obedience which Abraham and Moses, David and Solomon had struggled to attain in times past. In Jesus the new day, long awaited by the people of Israel, had finally dawned. But Jesus' perfect worship of God brought with it an unmasking of false prayer and self-seeking piety, just as inevitably as brilliant light necessarily clarifies or banishes darkness from its presence.

For example, with the solemnity and magnificence of Solomon's temple there came a natural pride in the beauty and excellence of the worship offered there to God. And with elaboration of services arose a tragic arrogance on the part of a praying elite who felt contempt for the poor and less educated who could not very often afford to quit work to join in the many religious festivals and observances in Jerusalem. Jesus' own prayer, in Luke 10:21,23f., reflects this situation and his response to it:

> In that same hour he rejoiced in the Holy Spirit and said, "I thank thee, Father, Lord of heaven and earth, that thou hast hidden these things from the wise and understanding and revealed them to babes; yea, Father, for such was thy gracious will. . . ." Then turning to the disciples he said privately, "Blessed are the eyes which see what you see! For I tell you that many prophets and kings desired to see what you see, and did not see it, and to hear what you hear, and did not hear it."

In this prayer Jesus draws a contrast between the "wise and understanding"—who were the professional clergy of his day and the learned teachers of religion—and the babes, his own disciples with all their faults and inexperience.

It was perhaps inevitable for King Solomon to paint God in his own image, as a greater King with greater wisdom and power, requiring a royal temple with courtly clergy to officiate at ceremonious worship for his greater glory. But Jesus' own experience of God as Father radically changed that theology of worship. If God is best understood as our Father, then we are his children, members of his family, and to begin with, babes. Just as a building does not make a home, but rather the quality of personal relationships that occur and grow within the walls, so too blessedness in God's worship does not come from the costly appointments of an imposing temple nor from pride of learning or height of position in the religious hierarchy. Supreme happiness comes from the humility to see God as our Father and to hear Jesus' words about God's rule already at work and present in our midst.

An unforgettable illustration of Jesus' stress upon humbleness as a first step toward fruitful prayer is found in Luke 18:11f., where the temple is pictured, and in it two men at worship. The first was a proud Pharisee, who thanked God that:

> I am not like other men, extortioners, unjust, adulterers, or even like this tax collector. I fast twice a week, I give tithes of all that I get.

Although the words of that prayer may have been quite true literally, they did not establish communication with God, nor did they bring about growth for the devout Pharisee. At best they were a fairly innocuous form of pious self-gratification.

In vivid contrast, the despised tax collector, the second actor in this drama, stood far off by himself in his shame, and "would not even lift up his eyes to heaven, but beat his breast, saying, 'God, be merciful to me a sinner!'" (Lk 18:13f.), and he it was who went home justified, accepted and blessed by God. Here is surely the other side of the coin. The value and appropriateness of temple worship is assumed. The glorious psalms of David are to be sung in the temple, and in its courts the wisdom of Solomon and the Torah of Moses are to be taught, but only in a spirit of humility and reverence. If liturgy turns into pomposity, or if learning becomes contempt for others, they lose their goodness and destroy the prayer and worship for which they exist.

Likewise in Jesus' dramatic cleansing of the temple, recorded in Luke 19, he drove out those who had turned the courts of the Lord into a den of robbers by their money-changing tables and their business of selling pigeons, in themselves useful activities but, in greed for profit, destructive of the temple as a house of prayer. It is the spirit of worship, the intention of the prayer, the quality of the dedication which goes along with attendance at the house of God that determines who we really are in God's sight and how close we can approach our Father. As recorded in Luke 21:1–4, one day Jesus saw

> the rich putting their gifts into the treasury; and he saw a poor widow put in two copper coins. And he said, "Truly I tell you, this poor widow has put in more than all of them; for they all contributed out of their abundance, but she out of her poverty put in all the living that she had."

Prayer and worship, in other words, are not prestigious occupations, nor are they occasional activities to be fitted, when convenient, into imposing social calendars. For Jesus they are fundamental for all persons whatever their status, because nothing is more important for him than to grow in closeness to God our Father, so as to accomplish more fruitfully his will for us all, day by day.

MATTHEW'S ACCOUNT OF THE LORD'S PRAYER

Immediately after Jesus' baptism, he was tempted by the devil in the wilderness. It is remarkable that all three evangelists, who report this event in Jesus' life, say that the Holy Spirit who came upon Jesus at his baptism led or drove him at once to this confrontation with evil. It is as though Matthew, Mark, and Luke want to present us with a model, a typical picture of the heights and depths of Christian experience, and use the beginning of Jesus' public ministry as their starting point. They seem to say that our Lord knew both the exaltation of joyful inspiration at his baptism, as well as the intense struggle with evil, self-deception, and disillusionment that seem to go along with goodness and

73

try to pervert the vision of God we receive. Jesus overcame that wilderness experience of temptation. Then he called his first disciples to be with him in his ministry and taught them day by day so that they might finally share with him in the glory of the transfiguration and resurrection to come.

Matthew especially stresses this relationship between temptation, discipleship, and growth in the knowledge and worship of the Father in heaven. In Matthew 4 we are given the temptations of Christ, along with the call of the first disciples. Then in Matthew 5, 6, and 7 there is the Sermon on the Mount, where they begin at once to learn the meaning of discipleship. Just as Moses went up to a mountain top to receive his Torah from God for the people of Israel, so Jesus went up on a mountain to teach his disciples the Beatitudes, his parables, right conduct, in fact his own Torah. And at the heart of the Sermon on the Mount, and at the center of Jesus' Torah, is the Lord's Prayer.[5]

The first chapter of the Sermon on the Mount ends with the challenge: "You, therefore, must be perfect, as your heavenly Father is perfect," a quality of life exemplified by a willingness to love one's enemies as well as one's neighbors, and a readiness to pray not only for friends but also for "those who persecute you" (Mt 5:44). With this reference to prayer, chapter 6 naturally leads into a discussion of true versus false worship: verses 1–4 contrast false ostentatious almsgiving to the offering of alms in secret, "and your Father who sees in secret will reward you." Likewise prayer should not be said in order to impress men, but should be done in private and with simplicity because "your Father knows what you need before you ask him" (Mt. 6:8).

Jesus' references here to praying in secret may remind the careful reader of Matthew's Gospel of what has been described some sixty-seven verses earlier in the temptations of Christ in the wilderness, where he was alone and fasting forty days and forty nights. The reader may also recall how Moses took, according to Exodus 34:28, was alone with the Lord forty days and forty nights, and fasting, before he delivered the Ten Commandments once more to the people of Israel.

The parallels, moreover, between Jesus' temptation and the content of the Lord's Prayer are very interesting. The first temptation of Christ was to question if he were truly the Son of God, and if so, to turn stones into bread to relieve his hunger. But the first words of the Lord's Prayer require that God really is our Father in heaven, that Jesus is indeed his Son, and that Jesus' disciples derive from their Lord the possibility of praying to God as their Father. Thus for Jesus there could be no "ifs" about his being God's Son. The forty days of prayerful reflection and profoundly serious worship enabled him to accept and affirm the vision he saw and the words he heard at his baptism as God-given. Having reached that decision and made that commitment, Jesus did not vacillate or agonize over it again.

Likewise, to try to use his authority and mission as God's Son to turn stones into bread would be a contradiction, for to be God's Son surely means to desire God's glory and not selfishly to seek one's own aggrandizement (like the hypocrites with their ostentation) or to act only for one's own benefit (like creating fresh bread from dry rocks to break the long fast). No! If God is our Father, then all our energy and intention must be to hallow his name, make it holy and blessed and honored in all we think and feel, say or sing, purpose and do. God, we may be sure, will give us in due season our daily bread; and our confidence, placed in him, suffices.

The second temptation of Christ is also paralleled by the Lord's Prayer; as Matthew 4:5ff. describes it:

> Then the devil took him to the holy city, and set him on the pinnacle of the temple, and said to him, "If you are the Son of God, throw yourself down; for it is written, 'He will give his angels charge of you,' and 'On their hands they will bear you up, lest you strike your foot against a stone.' " Jesus said to him, "Again it is written, 'You shall not tempt the Lord your God.' "

This is primarily a temptation to legitimate oneself, for Jesus to get for himself and his public empirical verification that he is really God's Son, irrefutable evidence by means of a spectacular leap from the top of God's house of prayer for everyone to see and marvel at. It is the temptation, as Paul would say, to be justified by works instead of trusting in one's justification by faith. For faith cannot put God to the test nor seek to force his hand. Never can faith demand from the Almighty a *quid pro quo,* an admission ticket, an ante before we let him join the game. For God is not made in our image. He is not a projection of earthly fathers nor a fantasy fabricated from indulgent grandmothers. Thus the evil of the second temptation is more insidious than the first, which only appealed to selfishness and pride. Here Jesus is tempted to make God into a tool, useful for Jesus' own ministry. The temptation is to cut God down to a convenient manageable size; to manipulate him; to manufacture from him different styles and shapes of god-packages which could cater to the religious market of the multicultural, bilingual society in which Jesus would be working.

It is also fascinating to note, as Shakespeare put it, how "the devil can cite Scripture for his purpose." Psalm 91:11f. is quoted to try to seduce Jesus into a suicidal leap; here the devil approaches the Bible as a collection of proof texts to justify his schemes. No attention is paid to the whole psalm; only two verses are cited from a total of sixteen. Of course these two verses do not make sense unless they are read in their context, but the tempter is not interested in the entire hymn, which begins with a glorious affirmation of trust in God, "my refuge and my fortress" (verse 2), and continues with many vivid illustrations of how the Lord is indeed our refuge (verse 9). The climax of this song of trust and praise is reached in verses 11–13, which are a splendid metaphor, having nothing to do with the literal Temple, but rather expressing the ecstatic faith that angelic help is nearby when evil threatens (verse 10), so we may move forward in our pilgrimage, being tripped up by no stones and, if necessary, being enabled to tread on lions or adders, and trample young lions or serpents underfoot rather than be deterred from going on in the accomplishment of God's will.

Obviously one does not literally trample a young lion underfoot (verse 13); this is a parabolical usage of language, but the devil is a literalist and cannot understand it. The devil also lacks humor. He did not appreciate the irony of Jesus' reply to his proof texts, when he cited Deuteronomy 6:16 against tempting the Lord your God, an allusion to the sin of the people of Israel in the wilderness, where they forced Moses to turn a dry rock into gushing water to satisfy their thirst. Here the devil is shown to be somewhat of a fool to think that Jesus might fall into the trap of trying to "put the Lord to the proof" (Ex 17:7). For

Jesus the wilderness was to be no mindless repetition of the bitter strife and failure of Moses' wilderness experiences. For Jesus it is sufficient to pray to his Father, "Lead us not into temptation, But deliver us from evil," and to act in accordance with such trust in his Father. Far from putting God to the test, our daily prayer must be that God will strengthen our confidence in him and our commitment to the tasks he gives us each day.

The third temptation is a desperate last effort of the devil to replace the coming of God's kingdom, and all the sacrifice and toil it would involve, with the easy, efficient, instant arrival of a kingdom, indeed "all the kingdoms of the world and the glory of them" (Mt 4:8). This quick route requires just one momentary detour from God's way—a brief worship of the devil—to achieve all that good. Matthew rightly recognizes that this is the climax of every temptation, the epitome of all seduction: to pretend that an evil, even an apparently small one, can be a shortcut to a more distant, arduous good. For a good end never justifies an evil means; a movement toward hell, or even a modest genuflection to the devil, can never be made right by a noble cause. If the devil personifies all that is sinful and in opposition to God, then whatever act of evil is committed, no matter how small it appears, can only take you that much farther in the wrong direction, away from God and your true homeland. Every brief detour is a dead end. There are no freeways on the road to righteousness, and to abiding joy there is no easy, instant access.

It is intriguing that the devil tries to start from the premise that all the earth is under his control. Here again the folly of the tempter is revealed, for in his absurd pride he has forgotten Psalm 24:1,

> The earth is the Lord's and all the fulness
> thereof,
> the world and those who dwell therein;

or the words of Isaiah 66:1,

> Thus says the Lord: "Heaven is my throne
> and the earth is my footstool. . . ."

The only possible reply which can be made to the pretentious drivel of the last temptation is given at once without further palaver in Matthew 4:10:

> Begone, Satan!
> "You shall worship the Lord your God and him only
> shall you serve."

For to worship Satan would be absolutely contradictory to Jesus and his mission of loving his Father and teaching his disciples how to share in that love. Thus it was in the Lord's Prayer that the disciples were taught to say, day by day, "Thy kingdom come" to our Father in heaven. Never can we bring about the kingdom of God by trafficking with the devil or by shady business arrangements with the forces of evil. Only light can give light and bestow illumination for our way; to think that you can make a deal with darkness to achieve quick enlightenment is simply crazy.

But it is no easy task to keep one's clarity of vision and personal integrity as a child of God. After Jesus' time of temptation, Matthew 4:11 concludes with the comment:

> Then the devil left him, and behold, angels came and
> ministered to him.

79

The battle for right was long, and the struggle was wearisome to worship and serve God alone. Nonetheless, one is never isolated in that great contest. As Hebrews 12:1f. puts it:

> Therefore, since we are surrounded by so great a cloud of witnesses, let us also lay aside every weight, and sin which clings so closely, and let us run with perseverance the race that is set before us, looking to Jesus the pioneer and perfecter of our faith, . . .

In summary, Jesus' own vocation as the Son of God became articulate and operative for him while he was at prayer after his baptism. Worship of God was the spark and catalyst that started Jesus on his ministry in which the full power and glory of God's kingdom became manifest for him and his disciples. Jesus' understanding of being God's Son did not come automatically with his birth. Luke seems to warn us that being a Son of God is a gift that comes by God's grace and is only to be recognized at our baptism and when that act of incorporation into the people of God and commitment to his ways is extended and ratified day by day by prayer and deepening worship of our Father in heaven. To be a Son of God and to pray with Jesus to our Father in heaven, Matthew shows us, is both a glorious vocation and an ongoing challenge. Temptations will follow, beginning with sordid occasions for self-indulgence, egotistical aggrandizement, and all the tediously absurd repertoire of sin, ending up with blasphemous worship of Satan himself. If, however, the love and worship of God is paramount in all we intend and do, then our sonship is assured and we may indeed pray with Jesus, as he taught his disciples—Our Father who art in heaven, . . .

THEMES FOR REFLECTION AND DISCUSSION

1. Luke is both the evangelist of prayer and of church music, with his famous canticles, such as the Song of Mary (1:46–55) and the Song of Simeon (2:29–32), to name only two examples. When Simeon said, or when we sing "Lord, now lettest thou thy servant depart in peace, . . ." that prayer was not only appropriate at the first time he used his words, but it has also remained meaningful in countless situations later on in the lives of others who have made Simeon's faith their own. The poetical form of the words and the musical setting in which they are frequently expressed illustrate an important aspect of worship: that it is often less discursive than affective; it is not always literal or prosaic, but on the contrary is frequently poetical, intuitional, and metaphorical. That is, prayer is not primarily an intellectual exercise, but rather an expression of the whole person, of thoughts, feelings, intentions, memories, and dreams. Are you able to use your whole personality in worship? As Jesus put it in reply to the scribe's question: "You shall love the Lord your God with all your heart, and with all your soul, and with all your mind, and with all your strength" (Mk 12:30).

2. Does the stress upon private prayer in Matthew 6 rule out or minimize the value of formal prayer in church? Is liturgical worship with many prepared prayers written ahead of time less authentic than spontaneous prayer in small groups or alone? These questions are often answered by saying that our intention in prayer and worship is more important than the form or style they take for their expression. Ideally, corporate liturgical prayer should balance and correct the excessive individualism and subjectivism that can distort private prayer and make it tend toward

self-gratification and wishful thinking rather than pure worship of God. On the other hand, personal spontaneous prayer saves formal worship from degenerating into hypocrisy or religious theatrics. If this answer is right, how do you keep the balance in your own life of prayer?

3. The legend is told about two strangers who approached the medieval town of Augsburg and saw a great swarm of demons going into an imposing building at the edge of the old city wall. They wondered what on earth could attract so many evil spirits and messengers of Satan. Was it the town brothel, the boardroom of the biggest bank, the backroom of the Bürgermeister? They found a citizen to ask about the building, and he said that it was the monastery of the Holy Spirit, whose monks were famous for their piety, learning, and many charitable works. Is it true that the more seriously the will of God is taken, the greater will be the temptations we have to face and overcome, lest we be perverted and destroyed?

OPTIONAL LENTEN STUDY GUIDE

1. The Fourth Sunday in Lent can be celebrated with this Collect:

> Gracious Father, whose blessed Son Jesus Christ came down from heaven to be the true bread which gives life to the world: Evermore give us this bread, that he may live in us, and we in him; who lives and reigns with you and the Holy Spirit, one God, now and for ever.[6]

Note that we speak of Jesus Christ as the gracious Father's blessed Son, who came down from heaven "to be the true bread which gives life to the world." While the words and deeds of Jesus are surely "food for thought," the reference here is primarily to the Eucharist, where we remember and participate in the Last Supper with Jesus and his first disciples. The prayers of the Eucharist are a sublime expression and expansion of Jesus' words and actions in his fellowship meals with his new family of friends and disciples, just as Jesus himself took the old Passover blessings and prayers of thanksgiving over bread and wine, and reinterpreted them for his followers as a way of understanding his own sacrificial death. Prayer for Jesus had this living flexibility, a vitality that could accept the good in past worship and redirect it to a greater good in the present. Are we as flexible with new prayer books and contemporary forms of worship?

2. The location of worship for Jesus also provides a helpful model for his disciples today. While not seeking to destroy the temple but rather cleanse it of commercialism and self-centeredness, Jesus had a more personal, family-like understanding of prayer than did the temple authorities of his day, who modeled their worship on the royal court of King Solomon. For Jesus, who addressed God as Father, a relaxed, family meal became the most natural context for worship of our Father, and an informal walk with friends, the members of his new family, became an occasion to "consider the lilies of the field, how they grow; they neither toil nor spin; yet . . . even Solomon in all his glory was not arrayed like one of these" (Mt 6:28f.). Many of the new worship books and liturgies recently introduced in numerous Christian churches provide a wide variety of new services which express this less courtly understanding of prayer and are suitable for family and private use at home or even under a tree in the backyard or in a park or any other place of quiet reflection. Examples from The Proposed Book of Common Prayer would include the new

Noonday Prayer (p.103), the Order of Worship for the Evening (p.108), Compline (p.127), and Daily Devotion for Individuals and Families (p.137). There is also a fine large collection of individual prayers and thanksgivings (p.810–841), covering the whole range of Christian life and practice, appropriate both for use in formal church services and for private use away from church buildings.

3. The form of the Lord's Prayer in many of the new prayer books differs from its traditional language because of a widespread concern to render the English of the prayer as faithfully as possible to the original Greek of the ancient texts, and to use words which would be as close as feasible to those used by other English-speaking Christian groups. For example, in The Proposed Book of Common Prayer, the translation is much indebted to the extensive work done by the International Consultation on English Texts, a group of twenty-five representatives from Roman Catholic, Anglican, Presbyterian, Lutheran, Baptist, Methodist, and Congregational Churches. The greatest change in the new translation of the prayer is the use of the words "Save us from the time of trial," which replace the old form, "Lead us not into temptation." The old petition, in fact, seemed to contradict James 1:13, "Let no one say when he is tempted, 'I am tempted by God.' " The new language more accurately expresses the intention of the Greek: to be a petition for help when the final onslaught and woes come upon us. Do you resent or approve of such change in traditional forms of prayer? What does your resentment or approval tell you about your understanding of the nature of religious language and its best use in prayer?

V

THE OLD TEMPLE AND
THE NEW SPIRIT OF PRAYER

PETER

Luke is unique among the members of the early Church, for he wrote both a Gospel about the life and teaching of Jesus, and the Acts of the Apostles, which showed the impact of Jesus upon his disciples after his death and resurrection. Just as Luke wanted to stress the importance of prayer for Jesus' own development and full realization of his ministry, so too in Acts we find prayer and worship a recurring theme, both as the prerequisite for effective action, and the inspiration and source of strength necessary to persevere and bring the mission of the Church to fruition. For example, Luke's Gospel ends with the disciples, after their commissioning by the risen Lord, remaining in Jerusalem with great joy, "continually in the temple blessing God." Their joyous worship was caused by their knowledge of Jesus' victory over death and by his promise to send them "power from on high," a reference to the gift of his Spirit (Lk 24:49).[1] Luke's second volume, the Acts of the Apostles, begins with this same motif, the return of Peter and the other brethren to the upper room where they were staying in Jerusalem (1:14):

> All these with one accord devoted themselves to prayer, together with the women and Mary the mother of Jesus, and with his brothers.

Jerusalem had been known for centuries as Zion, "my holy hill," as God was said to have called it in Psalm 2. It was on the holy hill of the Lord that the earliest Christian community assembled in expectancy and worship, and began to move forward in self-understanding and articulation of its faith and mission. One of the first acts of the young Church was to reflect upon Judas' betrayal of the Lord, and to interpret his action in the light of Scripture, particularly with Psalms 69:25 and 109:8 in mind. If that upper room where they were staying (Acts 1:13) was the same upper room used for the Last Supper (Lk 22:12), where Jesus and his disciples had celebrated the Passover, in which he remembered the past action of God recorded in Scripture and applied it to the present, then Peter and his companions might very naturally have been predisposed to attempt to do the same thing, when in their worship together they came to parts of the prayer book of Israel, where words seemed extremely relevant to their new situation. Peter himself might particularly have applied the words of Psalm 69:1ff. to himself:

> Save me, O God!
> For the waters have come up to my neck.
> I sink in deep mire,
>   where there is no foothold;

> I have come into deep waters,
>   and the flood sweeps over me.
> I am weary with my crying;
>   my throat is parched.

Surely Peter's first pain and remorse over his denial of Jesus might have seemed to him like flood waters of despair about to drown him. Certainly he could say with the psalmist: "O God, thou knowest my folly; the wrongs I have done are not hidden from thee" (69:5). Only after Jesus' resurrection and appearance to Peter could these words take on new meaning for him, as his guilt was forgiven and his shame gave way to the joy of Easter.

But as this great psalm may have continued in use by Jesus' disciples in worship together, other parts of Psalm 69 might well have served to express the feelings and actions of other persons as well. For Jesus himself verse 9 would come to be recognized as supremely appropriate: "Zeal for thy house has consumed me, . . ." and surely the words of verse 21 would have seemed in time to be an amazing anticipation of what had happened at the crucifixion: "for my thirst they gave me vinegar to drink." So, too, the bitter curse of the psalmist against his enemies had an uncanny relevance when applied to Judas: "May their camp be a desolation, let no one dwell in their tents." These words from Psalm 69:25 are quoted by Peter in the first chapter of Acts as an explanation of the meaning of the extraordinary death of Judas, who fell headlong and burst open, making a field of blood as he lay dying (Acts 1:18ff.).

But not only desolation came with Judas' death, but also an incentive to action. In Acts 1:20, Peter went on in his exhortation to the brethren to cite the Greek words of Psalm 109:8, "His office let another take," or more literally translated, "let someone else take his office of overseer," in Greek, his *episcopate*.[2] It is remarkable that this reading of Psalm 109:8 is only possible when the Greek version of the Psalter is used, the earlier Hebrew text suggesting a different idea. Thus Luke implies that already in the earliest days of the new Church Christian worship and preaching could take place in more than one language. Both the traditional Hebrew of the old sacred Scriptures and the new, more easily understood translation of the Old Testament into the Greek of popular commerce, education, and international travel were acceptable vehicles for the self-understanding of the Church and the proclamation of the Gospel to others. It was a great step forward to recognize that God was a good linguist and could be addressed not only in the old ceremonious language of Israel but also in the *Koine*, the common language of the eastern Mediterranean world. Notable too is the concern of the apostles to make up the loss in their number by the death of Judas, so as to continue both their ties with the historical life and teaching of Jesus, and their witness to his resurrection (Acts 1:21f.).

The prayer of Peter and the brethren as to whether Matthias should replace Judas is also illuminating. In Acts 1:24f., Luke reports:

> And they prayed and said, "Lord, who knowest the hearts of all men, show which one of these two thou hast chosen to take the place in this ministry and apostleship from which Judas turned aside, to go to his own place."

This is the first prayer whose words are recorded in Acts, and already Jesus is addressed as Lord, just as earlier in Peter's exhortation Jesus was given that title (Acts 1:21). So, soon after the resurrection, we see the disciples coming to appreciate who Jesus was and is, and to apply to him in worship the name Lord, which in the Old Testament was a reverent title for God himself. Now is dawning a deeper appreciation of the wisdom and love of God, who is not only recognized as embracing the infinitely creative fruitfulness of male and female, but is also seen to present a human face to us in Jesus, our Lord.

After the selection of Matthias to replace Judas, Luke proceeds at once in the second chapter of Acts to describe the gift of the Holy Spirit to the new Church when it had assembled to celebrate the festival of Pentecost. Again language plays a decisive role in this story, where the mighty works of God are told and understood in a host of foreign tongues, reversing the curse of Babel, where mankind lost its unity and the ability to communicate with visitors and strangers from afar.[3] In his first sermon Peter explains the meaning of Pentecost as a fulfillment of Joel's prophecy that God would pour out his Spirit on all flesh (Acts 2:17), so that whoever calls on the name of the Lord shall be saved (verse 21), and that Lord is Jesus Christ (verse 36).

The success of Peter's words was extraordinary; some three thousand souls repented, were baptized, and awaited the gift of the Holy Spirit. As Luke concludes his description of the birthday of the Christian Church in Acts 2:42:

> They devoted themselves to the apostles' teaching and fellowship, to the breaking of bread and the prayers.

Here at the first celebration of Pentecost in the new Church, the universalism we have observed previously developing in the worship of Abraham, David, and Solomon comes to completion. While the first congregation and bystanders were predominantly Jewish, the worldwide out-

89

reach of the new faith was recognized as part of God's will for the Church. No nation or language should be considered alien or remain ignorant of the mighty acts of God in Jesus Christ. Every living person should have the chance to become part of Christ's fellowship and enjoy the new and exhilarating community with others which came from radically new reconciliation and closeness to God.

That a sense of newness is a characteristic mark of the life and worship of the first generation of Christians is illustrated vividly by the story of Stephen. He and his six friends were given a special ministry of service to the poor, according to Acts 6:4, so that the apostles could devote themselves full time to prayer and preaching. Stephen had a vigorous and fruitful ministry until he was unjustly attacked as a blasphemer and stoned to death, ostensibly because he had claimed that Jesus would destroy the temple and the customs of Moses (Acts 6:14). It is understandable how the wealth of the temple and the pomp of its worship could have become repugnant to Stephen as he sought to serve widows and other impoverished, neglected folk. As he was suffering and dying from the wounds inflicted upon him by the hostile crowd, Stephen prayed (Acts 7:59f.).

> "Lord Jesus, receive my spirit." And he knelt down and cried with a loud voice, "Lord, do not hold this sin against them." And when he had said this, he fell asleep.

Stephen's prayer is reminiscent of the forgiving words of Jesus from the cross: "Father, forgive them; for they know not what they do (Lk 23:34). Both Stephen and Jesus have a new attitude of forgiveness, very different from that of the dying martyrs of Israel, celebrated in 2 Maccabees 7:16f., 19,31, who said to their tormentors and executioners:

> Do not think that God has forsaken our people. Keep on,
> and see how his mighty power will torture you and your
> descendants! . . . Do not think that you will go unpun-
> ished for having tried to fight against God! . . . You, who
> have contrived all sorts of evil against the Hebrews, will
> certainly not escape the hands of God.

New also was Stephen's understanding of worship, which
enraged his compatriots. The major part of Acts 7 is devoted to his sermon before the high priest. After recalling
the opening chapter of the nation's history, when Abraham
left the lowlands of Mesopotamia in response to God's
promise, and founded a new nation that would worship
God "in this place" (verse 7, the holy hill of Zion), Stephen
went on to describe God's ongoing faithfulness to
Abraham's descendants until the time of Moses, who "was
beautiful before God" (verse 20). "This is the Moses who
said to the Israelites, 'God will raise up for you a prophet
from your brethren as he raised me up' " (verse 37); with
these words Stephen refers to Jesus as the prophet who
would come, God's Righteous One (verse 52). But the Israelites refused both Moses and Jesus; and their most pow-
erful king, Solomon, made the tragic mistake of presuming
to build the temple, a house for God. In Acts 7:48ff., Stephen's testimony continues:

> Yet the Most High does not dwell in houses made with
> hands; as the prophet says, "Heaven is my throne, and
> earth my footstool. What house will you build for me,
> says the Lord, or what is the place of my rest?"

Because Jesus had sought to cleanse the temple, without
success, and instead had been handed over by the temple
authorities for execution, Stephen says now, in effect, that

the old temple, the traditional sacrifices, and the courtly worship is passé, irrelevant, irremediable—indeed worse, repugnant to God. What is needed, and indeed what is at hand, now that the rejected Jesus has been vindicated and is standing at the right hand of God (verse 56), is a totally new order of worship and life in his Holy Spirit.

John was to make the same point as he remembered and described Jesus' conversation with the woman of Samaria who, in John 4:20–24, said about the temple on Mount Gerizim:

> "Our fathers worshiped on this mountain; and you say that in Jerusalem is the place where men ought to worship." Jesus said to her, "Woman, believe me, the hour is coming when neither on this mountain nor in Jerusalem will you worship the Father. You worship what you do not know; we worship what we know, for salvation is from the Jews. But the hour is coming, and now is, when the true worshipers will worship the Father in spirit and truth, for such the Father seeks to worship him. God is spirit, and those who worship him must worship in spirit and truth."

The past glory of Israel is undeniable: Abraham, Moses, David, Solomon are our fathers; "salvation is from the Jews." But that great chapter is over, and only to look backward with pride or nostalgia is pernicious and futile. Now is the hour when true worshipers may approach the Father in the way he wishes to be worshiped, in spirit and in truth.

In other words, with Jesus' ministry, death, and resurrection, something radically new has taken place, what Paul was to call the new creation. Chapters 14–17 of John record a farewell discourse and a prayer of Jesus for his disciples in which he encourages them to look forward to the coming presence and inspiration of the Counselor, the Holy Spirit, who will complete Jesus' ongoing mission in his Church. And after the resurrection, the Gospel of John records Jesus' challenge to Peter to "feed my sheep," no matter where that ministry might lead him, as he followed his Lord (21:15–19). Soon the old nationalistic prejudices would be forgotten as Jesus' disciples moved forward to bring about and embrace a worldwide fellowship of faith in the risen Christ.

Thus Acts 10 describes what may be called a Gentile Pentecost. It deals with the conversion of Cornelius, "a devout man who feared God with all his household, gave alms liberally to the people, and prayed constantly to God" (verse 2), and the liberation of Peter from his traditional Jewish fear of contamination by contact with non-Jews. Peter was willing to move away from the prejudices of his upbringing and to open his eyes to new possibilities. Responding to a vision he had while at prayer (verses 9–16), Peter went to Cornelius and said (verses 28f.):

> You yourselves know how unlawful it is for a Jew to associate with or to visit any one of another nation; but God has shown me that I should not call any man common or unclean. So when I was sent for, I came without objection. I ask then why you sent for me.

Cornelius explains how his prayer had been heard, and in a vision had been told to send for Peter to learn what he had to say. And Peter rose to the occasion. He began his fine message about the Good News of Jesus by saying: "Truly I perceive that God shows no partiality, . . ." (verse 34). His sermon ended when the Holy Spirit descended on all who heard him, the prejudices, boundaries, exclusions, and fears of men being broken down by this new creative act of God. If Pentecost in Acts 2 marks the reversal of the curse of Babel, this Gentile Pentecost in Acts 10 completes that restorative process with a new creation, when once more God says "let there be . . ." and his Spirit hovers over the chaos of men's anxiety and hostility, bringing fresh forgiveness, invigorating amazement, rejuvenating joy, and rich new fellowship.

The new spirit at work in the apostolic Church is also illustrated by two fine stories in Acts 8. Here prayer and worship are shown taking on a new dimension and having an exciting relevance to the concerns of everyday life. The sacred is no longer boxed up in a solemn building, the temple in Jerusalem, but is bursting forth, inspiring and illuminating both Jews and Gentiles, persons of high and low estate. For example, the Samaritans, so long despised by the elite of Jerusalem, received the word of God, and the apostles sent Peter and John to them. They prayed for the Samaritans, laid their hands on them, and they too received the Holy Spirit. No longer were those northerners damned by their southern neighbors as half-breeds and worthless. The old liturgical prejudices, social differences, and issues of churchmanship were crumbling before the new spirit in the land (Acts 8:14–17). Or take the dry desert road to Gaza, where an Ethiopian, a eunuch, the chief financial minister of Queen Candace, was shown the connection between the ancient Scriptures of Isaiah about the suffering servant of the Lord, and the Good News of Jesus. This alien and ostracized Ethiopian sought and was given Christian baptism, and so he began a new life of hope and joy (Acts 8:26–40).

This fresh approach to life and worship also forms an

impressive part of 1 and 2 Peter. The Ethiopian eunuch, impotent, and by Jewish law an outcast, nonetheless became so reconciled to God and to his own destiny when he saw the vital relationship between Isaiah's suffering servant, the life of Jesus, and his own situation, that he could go on his way rejoicing as a new man, now acceptable to God and in fellowship with God's people. Likewise, in 1 Peter 4:12f., the apostle wrote to his friends and fellow disciples of Christ:

> Beloved, do not be surprised at the fiery ordeal which comes upon you to prove you, as though something strange were happening to you. But rejoice in so far as you share Christ's sufferings, that you may also rejoice and be glad when his glory is revealed.

The "fiery trial" is an allusion to persecutions; indeed Nero is said to have burned Christian martyrs tied to stakes in his garden to illuminate his evening revelries. Now, however, because who Jesus was and is, even such appalling and agonizing tribulation does not invalidate life's meaning nor repudiate God's purpose for us. Christ himself suffered and died for his faith in God our Father in heaven. Failure, frustration, emptiness, and death itself now have meaning and value; the depths of hell itself have been illuminated and redeemed by the cross of Christ and the resurrection hope.

Long ago Psalm 139:7–10 asked:

> Whither shall I go from thy Spirit?
> Or whither shall I flee from thy presence?
> If I ascend to heaven, thou art there!
> If I make my bed in Sheol, thou art there!

> If I take the wings of the morning
>> and dwell in the uttermost parts of the sea,
> even there thy hand shall lead me,
>> and thy right hand shall hold me.

That beautiful language of hope found fulfillment in the Good News in 1 Peter 1:3ff.:

> Blessed be the God and Father of our Lord Jesus Christ! By his great mercy we have been born anew to a living hope through the resurrection of Jesus Christ from the dead, and to an inheritance which is imperishable, undefiled, and unfading, kept in heaven for you, who by God's power are guarded through faith for a salvation ready to be revealed in the last time.

This exuberant and exhilarating language comes to its climax in 2 Peter 1:3f., which speaks of Jesus our Lord: "his divine power has granted to us all things that pertain to life and godliness"; he has "called us to his own glory and excellence"; he has granted us that we may "become partakers of the divine nature." What happened at Jesus' transfiguration is a real possibility for his disciples today. The author of this work, probably a disciple writing in Peter's name some time after his death, looks back to Peter's experience on the mount of transfiguration and recalls (2 Peter 1:16ff.):

> We did not follow cleverly devised myths when we made known to you the power and coming of our Lord Jesus Christ, but we were eyewitnesses of his majesty. For when he received honor and glory from God the Father and the voice was borne to him by the Majestic Glory, "This is my beloved Son, with whom I am well pleased,"

we heard this voice borne from heaven, for we were with
him on the holy mountain.

No myths for 2 Peter, not even the vision of the Good as
described in Plato's myth of the cave. Because of the richly
meaningful and deeply personal fellowship of the apostolic
church, the author of 2 Peter appears to have felt so close
to Peter the apostle, and through him to the transfigured
Christ, that he could write in their name and power (3:18).

> Grow in the grace and knowledge of our Lord and Savior
> Jesus Christ. To him be the glory both now and to the day
> of eternity. Amen.

These are some of the last words written in the historical
development of the New Testament. Their challenge to
grow epitomizes the new spirit which gave birth to the
Christian Church, a spirit of movement forward, new freedom in the grace of Jesus, fresh knowledge of the Lord and
Savior. A fitting shout of thanksgiving and rejoicing are the
words "To him . . . the glory," and as the last word, *Amen,*
the ancient Aramaic exclamation used so often by Jesus,
meaning "truly is it so . . . so be it!"

PAUL

If many of the first Christians described in Acts and the
other writings from the apostolic Church present an impressive variety of new styles and theologies of worship,
Paul more than any other figure in the early Christian community embodies the fresh spirit of prayer that invigorated
the first disciples of the risen Lord.[4] To begin with, Paul
fully shared the old attitude toward the temple in Jerusalem, and made it the focal point of his legalistic and exclu-

sive understanding of worship: for him Zion was indeed God's holy hill and only in Jerusalem under the guidance of the temple authorities could the Lord be appropriately worshiped. Acts 8:1 records that Paul, first known as Saul, was present and consenting to Stephen's martyrdom, and Paul remembered later on with shame, in Galatians 1:13,23f., how he had persecuted the Christian Church.

The account of Paul's conversion to the new way of faith and worship in the Spirit is vividly described in Acts 9:3–19. Paul, journeying on his way to Damascus to arrest disciples of Jesus, is suddenly surrounded by a brilliant light, and he falls to the ground. Hearing the words "Saul, Saul, why do you persecute me?" he answers the heavenly voice with a question, "Who are you, Lord?" (verse 5). In another account of this experience (Acts 22:10), Paul goes on to ask Jesus "What shall I do, Lord?" The rest of Paul's dramatic change of belief and life style is well-known; but in terms of prayer and worship, Paul's response to the call of the risen Lord with questions is very interesting. It differs, for example, from the prompt response of Isaiah to the question he heard addressed to him during worship in the temple, "Who will go for us?" Isaiah said simply, "Here am I! Send me (Is 6:8). Likewise the boy Samuel learned to reply to the call of the Lord with a prompt "Speak, for thy servant hears" (1 Sam 3:10). Paul, in contrast, had to ask questions; he found himself in the dark, blind, and he had to be led by the hand to Damascus.

Similarly, the prayer of Ananias, who was to heal Paul, is far from automatic. Ananias responded to a vision with the words "Here I am, Lord," but raised some questions as to his mission to go lay his hands on the persecutor of the Church (Acts 9:10–17). The vision continued with a further command to go, along with a description of what the persecutor could become, a chosen instrument of the Lord, a new man who would suffer much for Christ's sake. The story ends with action: Ananias laid his hands in the name of the Lord Jesus on Saul, and spoke to him as to a brother; Saul received his sight, and more, the Holy Spirit and Christian baptism, not to mention food, for he had been fasting for three days (Acts 9:9,17ff.).

Like Jesus' struggle in prayer on the Mount of Olives (Lk 22:39–46), prayer for Paul could never again be mechanical or easy. Now it increasingly involved awkward questions, conflicting courses of action, contradictory opinions, and required of each individual a radically new seriousness and sense of personal commitment to understand and then implement God's will. When Jesus taught his disciples to pray "Thy kingdom come," that meant for them undreamed of responsibility and effort, as well as unprecedented delight. And like Jesus' long fast after his baptism, Paul too found physical discipline by fasting to be an important part of worship. So, for example, in Acts 14:22f., on the first missionary journey, we find Paul and Barnabas:

> . . . strengthening the souls of the disciples, exhorting them to continue in the faith, and saying that through many tribulations we must enter the kingdom of God. And when they had appointed elders for them in every church, with prayer and fasting they committed them to the Lord in whom they believed.

The other journeys of Paul recorded in Acts present further insights into the new understanding of prayer as it developed in the early Church, as not only deeply serious but also refreshingly humane and liberatingly flexible in its many forms of expression. For example, on the second journey Paul and his companion reach Philippi (Acts 16:13ff.), the first town of the West to hear of the message of the Lord Jesus. Paul's friend recalls their first sabbath in the district of Macedonia:

> On the sabbath day we went outside the gate to the riverside, where we supposed there was a place of prayer; and we sat down and spoke to the women who had come together. One who heard us was a woman named Lydia, . . . who was a worshiper of God. The Lord opened her heart to give heed to what was said by Paul. And when she was baptized, with her household, she besought us, saying, "If you have judged me to be faithful to the Lord, come to my house and stay." And she prevailed upon us.

In Philippi, a leading city of the Roman colony, there was apparently no Jewish synagogue to be found, but that proved to be no reason to assume that public prayer and worship could not take place; rather it became an opportunity to break down old prejudices and to create new relationships. Centuries before, a riverside in Greece provided an occasion for memorable prayer by Socrates. (See p. 13f.)

When there was no synagogue or when that traditional house of study and worship proved to be inhospitable, as in the case of Paul on his visit to Thessalonica, he felt free to go on to the marketplace or even on to the Areopagus hill to preach Jesus and the resurrection (Acts 17:1–14, 17,19). In impressive words, Acts 17:22f.,27f. reports this famous address of Paul. It begins:

> Men of Athens, I perceive that in every way you are very religious. For as I passed along, and observed the objects

of your worship, I found also an altar with this inscription, "To an unknown god." What therefore you worship as unknown, this I proclaim to you. . . . He is not far from each one of us, for "In him we live and move and have our being"; as even some of your poets have said, "For we are indeed his offspring."

Far from his formerly exclusive attitude toward Mount Zion, the holy hill of the Lord, Paul found the freedom to speak his mind and share his convictions, even on Mar's Hill, the Areopagus! And far from being contemptuous of Greek religion, he even cites two Greek poets in his speech to illustrate his point and bring his audience as best he can to faith in the risen Christ, certainly a belief very different from the faith of Socrates and the worship of Hippolytus.

The important thing for Paul is the constant effort to express and share his faith wherever he could, even at the heart of Greek civilization; just as later he would preach his faith in Rome, the center of the Empire. No longer were there to be any off-limits for the praise of God; every hill on earth for Paul must become in time a holy hill of the Lord. What has Jerusalem to do with Athens, Mt. Zion with Mar's Hill? Everything! For Paul sees in Jesus and the resurrection a new creation in which the whole world can rejoice.

Toward the close of his third journey, Paul paid a farewell visit to the Church at Ephesus; Acts 20:36ff. recalls the scene:

He knelt down and prayed with them all. And they all wept and embraced Paul and kissed him, sorrowing most of all because of the word he had spoken, that they should see his face no more. And they brought him to the ship.

Likewise at Tyre, in Acts 21:5f., Paul and his companion sought out the disciples:

> And when our days there were ended, we departed and went on our journey; and they all, with wives and children, brought us on our way till we were outside the city; and kneeling down on the beach we prayed and bade one another farewell. Then we went on board the ship, and they returned home.

Now any assembly of fellow Christians makes for Paul a holy place of worship, be it in a home or at the synagogue, on the seashore or even in prison. A building is only a secondary convenience. And certainly the temple in Jerusalem could not serve much longer as a place for serious worship or fruitful preaching of the Good News of Christ, for Paul was seized in the temple, according to Acts 21:30, and indeed was about to be killed until the Roman tribune intervened and arrested him.

The rest of Paul's life was spent as a prisoner, and ends in Rome with Paul thanking God and taking courage because of the Christian brethren who came to meet him (Acts 28:15). He lived in Rome two years (Acts 28:30f.)

> and welcomed all who came to him, preaching the kingdom of God and teaching about the Lord Jesus Christ quite openly and unhindered.

For Paul the old temple brought imprisonment and threats of death; the new spirit of fellowship in Christ gave him courage and freedom, a worldwide family, and hope to the last.

Already in Paul's letter to the Romans, composed well before his imprisonment in Jerusalem, Paul had written that Israel had failed to do God's will by not moving forward with a living faith. Instead they looked back to the traditional laws and ceremonies and tried to work out all their demands. In Romans 9:33–10:1, Paul cites Isaiah 28:16,8:14f. to prove his point:

As it is written,
"Behold, I am laying in Zion a stone
    that will make men stumble,
a rock that will make them fall;
and he who believes in him will not be put to shame."
Brethren, my heart's desire and prayer to God
for them is that they may be saved.

In Romans 11:26f., Paul prays for the salvation of Israel, citing Isaiah 59:20f.,27:9, that they may find in Christ no longer a stumbling stone but rather the fulfillment of Isaiah's promises:

"The Deliverer will come from Zion,
he will banish ungodliness from Jacob";
"and this will be my covenant with them
when I take away their sins."

Thus Paul found no betrayal of the glorious heritage of Israel in Christ, but rather its perfection, completion, and end, so that there might be a new creation. For example, the old Passover, a national festival, became in Christ a worldwide fellowship meal: "for Christ, our paschal lamb, has been sacrificed (1 Cor 5:7). Now even Gentiles could partake of the Lord's Supper (1 Cor 11:17–34), as the new far-reaching community came into being. Indeed even the past history of Israel took on new dimensions for Christian faith. As our fathers passed through the sea and journeyed to the promised land of liberty, they should be understood as having been saved by a baptism and by supernatural food and drink; Paul sees that in fact "they drank from the supernatural Rock which followed them, and the Rock was Christ" (1 Cor 10:4)—no stumbling stone, but a rock of salvation. In time Christ would come to many new communities of faith, offering himself to them in baptism and in supernatural food and drink—the Eucharist.

The Greek term underlying this very ancient and widespread part of Christian worship is *eucharistia,* meaning in particular the Eucharist meal, but also the more general idea of thanksgiving.[5] And that quality of thankfulness and joy pervades all the letters of Paul. Again and again he begins his messages to his churches with *eucharistia,* a prayer of thanksgiving for them, for their growth and courage to move forward in faith and in the spirit of Christ, seeking his mind in all they did, and working out their own salvation with fear and trembling (Phil 2:5,12). One of Paul's earliest letters is a fine example of this new attitude; 1 Thessalonians 1:2f. begins:

> We give thanks to God always for you all, constantly mentioning you in our prayers, remembering before our God and Father your work of faith and labor of love and steadfastness of hope in our Lord Jesus Christ.

That Paul's *eucharistia,* his thankful attitude, was not merely euphoria but could be directly geared to concrete action is well illustrated by his letter to Philemon, where Paul begins with a beautiful expression of thanksgiving and prayer (4–7), but then intercedes for a runaway slave and suggests that his owner, Philemon, receive him back, "no longer as a slave but more than a slave, as a beloved brother . . . in the Lord" (verse 16).

Finally notice should be taken of the prayer written with Paul's own hand at the end of 1 Corinthians: *Maranatha!* Our Lord, Come! This ancient Aramaic prayer was well-known in the apostolic Church, coming from the earliest days when most of Jesus' disciples spoke the Aramaic of Palestine. Now Paul can add that Aramaic prayer to his letter written in Greek to the Church of Corinth. Here again the curse of Babel has been broken and the gap of cultures and tongues bridged. That prayer itself contains a play on words that expresses well the new spirit sweeping over the ancient world. One way to translate *Maranatha* is, Our Lord has come, as a statement of historical fact which made Christian faith and worship possible. But *Maranatha* can also be translated as a prayer: "Our Lord, come!" Paul found that the prayer was being answered, for the spirit of Jesus did come to him day by day to inspire and encourage him to the end of his life. And that prayer also looks forward to the great Day, to the End, when our Lord shall come in the fullness of his kingdom, power, and glory. *Maranatha!*

In summary, both Peter and Paul were forced to leave the worship of the old temple because it could not accept change nor the spirit of the risen Lord. Both had to leave familiar surroundings, as did their father Abraham. They, like Moses, worked to liberate God's people from a narrow, encapsulated past, so as to move on to a new land of promise, the whole world. Like David, they found prayer and worship their daily inspiration. And like Solomon, they depended on God's wisdom, which they identified with the spirit of Christ the Lord, to lead them forward in their worldwide mission.

THEMES FOR REFLECTION AND DISCUSSION

1. The attitude of Stephen and Paul toward the temple at Jerusalem naturally raises the issue of church construction today and the expenditure of church income on such things as buildings, organs, or stained glass. How do you feel about the setting for Christian prayer? Would you attend worship as regularly if it were in someone's home or in a simple public assembly room? Do your feelings and preferences help you understand better your own theology of prayer?

2. Along with impressive church plants are found the crew to run them: educated and ordained clergy, teaching colleagues, musicians, secretarial and financial associates, building and maintenance help. One effort to simplify this understanding of ministry and worship has been the worker priest movement in Roman Catholicism, the tent-making ministry in some Protestant Churches, and the nonstipendiary ministry in Anglicanism, where ordained clergy receive no salary from the church congregation they serve, but work full time at an ordinary job like other Christians. Think through what would happen if the clergy you know best were no longer to receive any income from church offerings. What would they do? What would you do? What changes would take place? For better? For worse?

3. With the current Pentecostal and charismatic revival in many churches, the life of the early Christian communities and their dependence upon the Holy Spirit has awakened special interest. How do you define these important terms: spirit, the Spirit, holy, the Holy Spirit? If you have some difficulty formulating a definition, think instead about your methodology. How do you go about clarifying a theological

concept? Where do you go first? To the Bible, a dictionary, a history book, a clergyman, your own individual experience, and/or the experience of your friends and family? The way you answer these questions will help you understand both the issue under consideration and yourself.

OPTIONAL LENTEN STUDY GUIDE

1. The Collect for the Fifth Sunday in Lent:

> Almighty God, you alone can bring into order the unruly wills and affections of sinners: Grant your people grace to love what you command and desire what you promise; that, among the swift and varied changes of the world, our hearts may surely there be fixed where true joys are to be found; through Jesus Christ our Lord, who lives and reigns with you and the Holy Spirit, one God, now and for ever.[6]

The petition, "Grant your people grace to love what you command and desire what you promise," expresses a fine balance between past commandment (Torah) and future promise in the unfolding of God's plan. The tragedy of the temple authorities who rejected Peter and Paul was that they only loved the past commandments and could tolerate no movement toward a future promise. On the other hand, in the 1960s some Christians became so desirous of being where the action was, which they interpreted as God's promise brought up to date, that they had little time for the past and traditional values in worship. Their error was to jettison prayer for social activism. We can learn from both positions, and the Collect may suggest to some that "true joy" will be had when we can keep a creative tension between the two interpretations of God's will, and take both into consideration as we respond to the needs and challenges of each new day.

2. One of the finest hymns in use today was written by the British publisher of the London edition of the *Detroit Free Press* in 1908; it begins:

> In Christ there is no East or West,
>   In him no South or North,
> But one great fellowship of love
>   Throughout the whole wide earth.
> In him shall true hearts everywhere
>   Their high communion find;
> His service is the golden cord
>   Close-binding all mankind.
> Join hands, then, brothers of the faith,
>   Whate'er your race may be!
> Who serves my Father as a son
>   Is surely kin to me.[7]

The hymn is usually sung to an old Negro melody, "I know the angel's done changed my name." Saul's name was changed to Paul, and his Gospel of a fellowship of love in Christ made possible for the first time a world in which East and West, North and South could find "high communion" and "join hands" as brothers.

3. The important question of patriotism, national allegiance, and loyalty to one's own heritage as a citizen of a particular state or country is raised by the universalism the apostolic Church came to embrace in response to Jesus' life and message. Paul agonized over the destiny of the Jews in Romans 9–11; so loyal was he to his national patrimony that he could wish himself accursed if only his kinsmen by race

would accept Christ(9:3). And when it came to finding a means to continue his ministry of preaching, he did not hesitate to invoke his Roman citizenship, as we are told in Acts 16,22,25. Yet Paul's primary commitment was to the Lord Jesus Christ, and he devoted much of his efforts to correlate and integrate the two loyalties. The United States has gone through a period of bicentennial celebrations, remembering with thankfulness the spirit of 1776. How do we as Christians and as citizens relate that spirit to the spirit of Christ, in whom "there is neither Jew nor Greek, . . . slave nor free, . . . male nor female. . . . but a new creation?" (Gal 3:28,6:15).

VI

THE ADVANCE
OF CHRISTIAN FAITH
AND WORSHIP IN THE WEST
AND IN THE EAST

THE FIERY ORDEALS OF ROME

Peter's first letter spoke of the fiery ordeal which was coming upon the Church, and it is generally thought that Peter himself lost his life during the persecutions of Nero in about A.D. 64. A popular legend tells of his effort to escape from Rome because of the hardships the Church there was suffering, until he met a stranger as he fled along the Appian Way. It was the risen Lord, who had once long ago called him to discipleship in Galilee by the lakeside. Peter asked him, *"Domine, Quo vadis?* Lord, Where are you going?"* Jesus replied, "To Rome to be crucified again." So Peter stopped his hurried journey; he thought and prayed, and finally realized where he should be going. He returned to Rome and remained there with Jesus' disciples in the fiery trial they had to endure, for that was where his Lord was to be found.

This story of the end of Peter's life is typical of the attitude of an impressive number of early Christians, who chose the way of suffering and even death as martyrs instead of compromising or forsaking their faith in Jesus and communion with him in worship and Christian fellowship. Perhaps the most famous example is that of Ignatius, the Bishop of Antioch. Antioch, in fact, had been the first place where the disciples of Jesus were called Christians (Acts 11:26). After Rome and Alexandria, it was the third largest city of the Roman Empire. It had served as home base for the missionary journeys of Paul. And like Paul, Ignatius had been arrested for his faith and was being sent to Rome under guard. While making the long journey, Ignatius was able to write seven letters to encourage the friends and churches he was leaving behind. These epistles have been preserved in a collection of writings which come immediately after the New Testament Scriptures; they are now called the *Apostolic Fathers,* and they make fascinating reading from this exceptionally early chapter of Church history.[1]

As Ignatius journeys in the steps of Peter and Paul, he is hopeful and at peace, feeling himself sustained by the prayers and affection of the Churches of the regions he travels through: Syria, Asia Minor, Rome itself. For example, he begins his letter to the Ephesians by calling the Church there "worthy of all felicitation," "blessed with greatness," "united and chosen through true suffering"; to them he sends "abundant greeting in Jesus Christ and in blameless joy." His letter is indeed full of joy, remarkable considering the circumstances of Ignatius, condemned to death by being thrown to wild beasts in the Colosseum. But his great predecessor in Antioch, Paul himself, had found confidence and joy in an equally adverse situation, when he wrote while imprisoned that he could rejoice and be full of courage that Christ would be honored in his body, whether by life or by death: "For to me to live is Christ, and to die is gain" (Phil 1:13,21). Likewise Ignatius, a younger contemporary of Paul, could write at the end of his letter to the Ephesians:

> If Jesus Christ permit me through your prayers and it be his will, . . . I will show you concerning the dispensation of the new man Jesus Christ, . . . his faith and his love, his suffering and his resurrection. . . . Remember me as Jesus Christ also remembers you. Pray for the Church in Syria, whence I am led a prisoner to Rome, being the least of the faithful who are there, even as I was thought worthy to show the honor of God. Farewell in God our Father and in Jesus Christ, our common hope.[2]

Paul looked back with admiration to Abraham as a guide to follow, saying of him "in hope he believed against hope, that he should become the father of many nations; . . ." (Rom 4:18). These words of Paul apply well, both to his own ministry and to that of Ignatius. Like Abraham and Paul, Ignatius also was called westward from familiar surroundings to a new and frightening destiny. Though that condemnation to Rome was ominous and finally fatal, Ignatius looked to his martyr's death as the crowning chapter of his life on earth, and the beginning of a yet more wonderful life with God. So he wrote to the Roman Church:

> I have gained my prayer to God to see your godly faces. . . . Grant me nothing more than that I be poured out to

God, while an altar is still ready, that forming yourselves
into a chorus of love, you may sing to the Father in Christ
Jesus, that God has vouchsafed that the bishop of Syria
shall be found at the setting of the sun, having fetched
him from the sun's rising. It is good to set to the world
towards God, that I may rise to him.[3]

If Abraham was prepared to sacrifice his own son, but
was spared that supreme test, Ignatius embraced his own
self-sacrifice upon the altar of pagan Rome. Not only by his
sound teaching and faithful ministry as Bishop of Syria, but
also by his action of total commitment as a martyr, Ignatius
sought to worship God and complete his mission, even in
a hostile city, far to the west, "at the setting of the sun." Yet
by dying in Rome, "setting to the world towards God,"
Ignatius was confident that he would rise eternally to his
Father in Christ Jesus, for him the greatest meaning and joy
life had to offer.[4]

Ignatius died for his faith during the persecutions of the
Emperor Trajan in about A.D. 107. A remarkable successor
of his to the martyr's crown was Justin, who also came from
the East and lost his life in Rome. Born in Samaria and
having taught for a considerable time in Ephesus, Justin
later moved to the capital of the Empire, where he established a Christian school. He was beheaded for his beliefs
in about 165 under the persecutions of Marcus Aurelius.[5]
In the year 202 another emperor, Septimius Severus, pro-
hibited conversions to Christianity; in the following year
Perpetua and her companions, who had prepared for baptism in the Church of North Africa, were executed in
the arena at Carthage.[6] A contemporary of these African martyrs was Quintus Septimius Florens Tertullian,
who wrote appeals for the toleration of Christianity and

sought to show that Christians were good citizens.

About three years before the martyrdom of Perpetua, Tertullian wrote the first full study in the early Church dealing with prayer in general and the Lord's Prayer in particular. Tertullian may have been a lawyer by profession; in any case his style is rhetorical and what he says is elegantly stated and full of theological reflection. For example, he begins by saying:

> Jesus Christ our Lord has marked out for the new disciples of the new covenant a new plan of prayer. For it was right that in this case, too, new wine should be stored in new bottles and a new patch be stitched on to a new garment. For everything that was aforetime has either been transmuted, like circumcision, or supplemented, like the rest of the Law, or fulfilled, like prophecy, or made perfect, like faith itself. The new grace of God has renewed all things from carnal to spiritual by the subsequent addition of the Gospel, the fulfiller of all older antiquity: for in it our Lord Jesus Christ is approved as God's Spirit and God's Word and God's Reason—Spirit in view of his power, Word in view of his teaching, Reason in view of his intervention. So therefore the prayer instituted by Christ is of three constituents, of word in that it is clearly spoken, of spirit in that it has great power, of reason in that it reconciles.[7]

Tertullian, who claimed that Jerusalem, the city of God, had nothing to do with Athens and pagan philosophy,[8] naturally regarded the prayer of Jesus as something radically new, just as Revelation 21:5, written during the persecutions of Nero and Domitian, pictured God on his throne, telling the Church, "Behold, I make all things new." For

Tertullian, the new grace of God has indeed renewed all things—and thus the Church needs elaborate sermons or tracts, such as Tertullian himself had composed, in order to understand the full implications of prayer, not to mention the need for wise teachers to encourage new Christians and to help the mature in the faith clarify their prayers and deepen their worship.

The parallel which can be drawn between Tertullian and Moses is intriguing, and it goes beyond the fact that they were both in their own ways lawyers. Both men represent an approach to worship which understands that an original revelation from God, be it the Ten Commandments or the Lord's Prayer, needs to be fleshed out in meditation and commentary, and then incarnated in concrete action. The Lord's Prayer became for Tertullian a treasury of theological principles which could be extended into all of life. Thus he claims that:

> We have the right, after rehearsing the prescribed and regular prayer as a foundation, to make from other sources a superstructure of petitions for additional desires: yet with mindfulness of the precepts, let we be as far from the ears of God as we are from the precepts.[9]

Tertullian goes on to argue that we cannot pray effectively if we are angry; a clean, ethical life is the prerequisite for prayer; one should stand to pray because the Gentiles sit down "after worshiping their puppets"; we should worship at least three times a day, "being the debtors of three, the Father, the Son, and the Holy Spirit," in addition to the other regular prayers each day.

115

The *Tract on the Prayer* by Tertullian ends with these stirring words of great rhetorical power:

> The old prayer, no doubt, brought deliverance from fire and wild beasts and hunger, while yet it had not received its pattern from Christ: then how much more fully operative is the Christian prayer! . . . Prayer is the bulwark of faith, our defensive and offensive armor against the enemy who is watching us from every side. So let us never proceed unarmed: by day let us remember the station, by night the vigil. Beneath the armor of prayer let us guard our Emperor's standard: let us pray while waiting for the angel's trumpet. Even the angels pray, all of them. The whole creation prays. . . . Even the Lord himself prayed: to him be honor and power for ever and ever.[10]

Tertullian's outstanding pupil was Cyprian, who became Bishop of Carthage about 248, and ten years later was executed for his faith during the persecutions of the Emperor Valerian. Like Peter in the *Quo vadis* legend, Cyprian at first eluded his persecutors, but hearing that Pope Sixtus had lost his life with his companions in the catacombs of Rome, he gave himself up, and was beheaded by the Roman authorities, the first African bishop who became a martyr.

Cyprian greatly revered his teacher Tertullian and his tract on prayer; Cyprian in fact decided to write his own treatise on the Lord's Prayer as an expansion and updating of Tertullian's work of some fifty years earlier, with further pastoral insights and reflection upon prayer. Cyprian's treatise lacks the brilliance—and brittleness—of Tertullian's study; instead of his predecessor's strongly apologetic and doctrinal tone, Cyprian on the Lord's Prayer is far more devotional and mellow in his approach: indeed it has been called the best work on the subject in the long history of Christianity,[11] and it is surely a delight to read.

For example, Cyprian reminds the Church that Christ himself

> gave the form of praying, himself advised and instructed us what to pray for. He who made us to live taught us also to pray. . . . What prayer can be more spiritual than that which was given us by Christ, by whom the Holy Spirit was sent to us, what prayer to the Father can be more true than that which was sent forth from the Son, who is truth, out of his mouth? . . . The Teacher of peace and master of unity did not wish prayer to be offered individually and privately as one would pray only for himself when he prays. We do not say: "My Father, who art in heaven," nor "Give me this day my bread, . . ." Our prayer is public and common, and when we pray, we pray not for one but for the whole people, because we, the whole people, are one. God, the teacher of prayer and concord, who taught unity, thus wished one to pray for all. . . .[12]

These words are especially impressive when the circumstances in which Cyprian lived are recalled: persecution, divisiveness over what to do with members of the Church who had given up their faith through fear of torture, and opposition to Cyprian's own ministry.

Worship and conduct are closely interrelated in Cyprian's teaching: "When we speak of God, we ought to act as sons of God. . . . Let us live as if temples of God, that it may be clear that the Lord dwells in us."[13] For Cyprian, the temple on God's holy hill in Jerusalem has become multiplied a thousandfold, indeed beyond imagination, for now each of us calls God Father and we all must become holy temples for his Holy Spirit. Here Cyprian extends to the shores of north Africa Paul's great doctrine in 1 Corinthians 6:19f.: "Do you not know that your body is a temple of the Holy Spirit within you? . . . So glorify God in your body."

THE NEW JERUSALEM

While these two centuries, from the death of Peter in about A.D. 64, during Nero's persecutions, to the martyrdom of Cyprian in 258, were a time of intense struggle and growth for the Church in the West, Christians in the East were also making remarkable advances both in the extension of Christian faith and in the deepening expression of their worship and commitment. After Jerusalem was destroyed in the Jewish War of 66–70, Caesarea, Antioch, and then Alexandria became centers of Christian activity and impressive growth.

But Jerusalem itself was a very different matter. Toward the end of the revolt, Titus, the son of the Roman Emperor, slowly starved the inhabitants of the city with his terrible siege. Eventually storming the center of the fortifications, he massacred everyone not already killed by famine and disease.[14] In the process of subduing the city, the temple caught fire and was destroyed. A few Jews continued to live in Jerusalem, but with no temple the Jewish religion gradually transformed itself into rabbinic Judaism, centered in synagogue worship and study of the Torah. Less than fifty years later there was another series of uprisings against Rome, leading to the revolt in the year 132 by Simon Bar-Cochba, who claimed to be the Messiah. When he was defeated in 135, all Jews were banished from Jerusalem, and on the site of the destroyed temple the Roman Legate set up statues of Zeus and the Emperor Hadrian. A Roman colony, called Aelia Capitolina, was built upon the ruins of the old Jerusalem. The traditional site of the tomb of Jesus was buried under earthwork for a temple of Aphrodite.[15]

Although the old Jerusalem was no more God's holy hill for Jews and Christians during this terrible time for the Holy Land, the new faith of Jesus' disciples advanced well in other cities; for example, in Caesarea, the capital of Palestine, the location of the "Gentile Pentecost" (Acts 10) and Paul's two-year imprisonment (Acts 24). Antioch has already been distinguished as the home of Ignatius, its bishop and martyr. Alexandria remains to be mentioned as the second city of the Roman Empire, which in fact had a larger Jewish community than Jerusalem itself.[16] Just as Justin came to Rome to establish a school for Christian instruction, so too in Alexandria by about the year 180 a famous catechetical school had been founded to extend Christian faith and practice among the educated.

The most illustrious of the teachers of this school was Origen, whose father had been killed during the persecution of 202. After working in Egypt as a biblical scholar and theologian, Origen moved in 231 to Caesarea, where he established another famous school. Living there a life of great personal piety and devoting himself to writing and preaching, he was imprisoned in 250 and subjected to prolonged torture during the persecutions of the Emperor Decius, from which he survived in failing health until his death in 254. Origen thus makes a fascinating parallel to Cyprian: both were contemporaries, both lived on the shores of north Africa, both suffered terrible persecution from the Roman government and endured bitter dissension within their own Churches, and both wrote at about the same time on the Lord's Prayer.

Origen's *Treatise on Prayer* is the most lengthy and detailed study of prayer we have considered. Origen more than any other early writer realized that prayer and worship were vastly important and unfathomable in their depths of meaning for Christians. Thus he began his great work:

> Things which cannot be grasped by rational and mortal kind because they are vast and superhuman, and far surpass our perishable nature, nevertheless by the will of God become capable of being so grasped by reason of the abundant and immeasurable grace of God poured out from him towards men through Jesus Christ, the minister of boundless grace towards us, and through the Spirit, his fellow-worker.[17]

By the grace of God we may come to understand the greatness of prayer—so Origen starts out; and after thirty-four chapters of profound reflection on the nature of prayer and the art of worship, he ends by asking his readers to pray for him that God would enlighten him further so he might write a second and better account about the great topic he has undertaken to study. That is, prayer for Origen is like the top of an enormous iceberg, or to use an analogy more appropriate to his homeland in Egypt, worship is like the apex of a huge pyramid: the more you know of it, the more you realize how far you have to go to comprehend its heights, depths, and tremendous gravity.[18]

Two examples must suffice from this treasure house of theological reflection. Origen suggests that serious prayer requires knowledge both of the proper method or art of prayer, as well as an appropriate subject matter in our prayers:

> It is necessary not only to pray, but also to pray as we ought, and to pray for what we ought. . . . One of these

two things, namely praying for what we ought, consists in the words of our prayer; the other, praying as we ought, consists in the disposition of him who prays. To illustrate this, the following passages show what we ought to pray for: Ask for the great things, and the small things shall be added unto you; and, Ask for heavenly things and earthly things shall be added unto you (*cf.* Mt.6:33); and, Pray for them which despitefully use you (Mt.5:44). . . . The following illustrates how we ought to pray: I will therefore that men pray everywhere, lifting up holy hands, without wrath and doubting. In like manner also, that women adorn themselves in modest apparel, with shamefacedness and sobriety . . . (I Tim 2:8ff.). . . . First be reconciled to thy brother, and then come and offer thy gift (Mt 5:23f.).[19]

The outstanding abilities of Origen as an interpreter of the Bible are seen in this excerpt. His understanding of prayer is rooted in Scripture and reflects firsthand and ongoing love and meditation upon God's word.[20]

A second illustration shows Origen's indebtedness to the Psalms of David, the prayer book of Israel. Origen refers to more than fifty psalms to illuminate his discussion of Christian prayer. For example, he writes that:

there are four sections [of prayer] to be described, which I have found scattered in the Scriptures, and we must each organize our prayer in accordance with them. These sections are as follows: according to our ability at the beginning and exordium of our prayer we must address praises to God through Christ, who is praised together with him in the Holy Spirit, who is likewise hymned; and after this each must place thanksgiving, both general— enumerating with thanksgiving God's benefits to the many—and for those things which each has received privately from God; and after thanksgiving it seems to me that one ought to be a bitter accuser of one's own sins before God, and to ask first for healing so as to be delivered from the state that leads to sin, and secondly for remission of what is past; and after confession, in the fourth place it seems to me we must add petition for the great and heavenly gifts for ourselves, and for people in general, and also for our families and friends; and in addition to all this, our prayer ought to end in praise to God through Christ in the Holy Spirit.[21]

Then he goes on to cite Psalm 104 as an example of praise, followed by David's thanksgiving (2 Sam 7:18–22), then Psalm 39:8 and Psalm 38:5f. as illustrations of confession, and finally Psalm 28:3 to exemplify petition. If David was the greatest psalmist of Israel, Origen was the outstanding Christian commentator upon David's prayer book in the early Church; no other author showed with such cogency and breadth of knowledge the relevance of Holy Scripture to the life of prayer.

While Origen stands for the high importance the early Church placed upon the Bible, a successor of his represents very well the other main emphasis in early Christianity, which was devotion to the sacraments and liturgical worship; his name is Cyril of Jerusalem. Born about sixty years after the death of Origen, Cyril's life marks the turning point in the attitude of the Roman government toward Christianity, for in the year 313 the Emperor Constantine recognized the right of the Christian churches to exist and agreed to tolerate all religions. Indeed Constantine in time came to support the small Christian community in what was left of old Jerusalem, now called Aelia, and after the Council of Nicaea, in 325, he agreed to remove the Temple of

Aphrodite to search for the tomb of Christ. Constantine decided as well to erect a great basilica in Jerusalem, as Eusebius of Caesarea reported,

> a church which, not only in its ensemble might surpass in loveliness all others, but also the details of which should be of such a quality that their excellence would transcend in beauty anything that the other cities of the Empire could show. . . .[22]

and around the tomb of Christ a splendid rotunda, "a sanctuary of a magnificence worthy of his wealth and of his crown." These buildings of Constantine became the first Church of the Holy Sepulchre. No longer was Jerusalem synonymous with treason and revolt against Rome; soon the small Roman colony of Aelia was to become a new Jerusalem, with a splendid basilica for pilgrims to worship in from all over the Empire.[23]

Little is known of Cyril's early life, but it is likely that he grew up in or near Jerusalem as the Christian community there became free to express its faith in open worship and public preaching. It became increasingly possible and desirable to remember and celebrate the historical events in Jesus' life, so closely connected with Jerusalem and nearby Bethlehem. For example, the custom developed in worship to commemorate the Presentation of Christ in the Temple, the Palm Sunday procession, and the Adoration of the Cross on Good Friday. These liturgical expressions of corporate prayer in Jerusalem were in time taken over by the Church in the West, and through the spread of the Roman rite became widely known and practiced in the ongoing worship of Christians.[24]

Cyril himself was much involved in this liturgical renaissance in Jerusalem, first as deacon, then as priest, and later as Bishop of Jerusalem. Few of his writings survive, save for his exceptionally valuable *Catechetical Lectures,* which he gave to his candidates preparing for baptism and to the recently baptized members of his Church. It is remarkable that Cyril gave his addresses in 350 in the great basilica built by the Roman emperor, when a century before Origen was being tortured not very far away during the persecutions of another Roman emperor.

In Cyril's first address to the baptismal candidates in the presence of the whole Church, the congregation is exhorted to:

> Pray yet more often that God will judge you worthy of heavenly and immortal mysteries. Cease not day or night, but when sleep falls from your eyes, then let your mind free itself to pray. . . . It is my part to tell you, yours to carry it forward, but God's to bring it to completion. Let us brace our minds, concentrate our souls, prepare our hearts. The race is run in matters of soul, and the prize consists of rewards in heaven.[25]

Here Cyril reminds his Church that prayer is serious work and involves disciplined use of the mind in thoughtful reflection. Since Christian discipleship for Cyril embraces the whole personality—mind, soul, and heart—we are held responsible to train and exercise all these faculties in running the race, the *curriculum* God has for each of us. And God is for us! He will bring our work to completion if we persevere in carrying it forward.

For Cyril, the crowning sign of incorporation into the life of the Church for new Christians is their reception of the

Eucharist. The last of Cyril's *Mystagogical Catecheses* gives us a moving insight into this high point of the worship of his community; coming after the profession of faith and baptism of the new members, it is called by Cyril "the finish to your spiritual edification." After describing and explaining the meaning of the opening greetings, prayers, and hymns of the Holy Eucharist, Cyril continues:

> Then having sanctified ourselves by these spiritual hymns, we call upon the merciful God to send forth his Holy Spirit upon the gifts lying before him; that he may make the bread the Body of Christ, and the wine the Blood of Christ; for whatsoever the Holy Ghost has touched, is sanctified and changed. Then, after the spiritual sacrifice is perfected, the bloodless service upon that sacrifice of propitiation, we entreat God for the common peace of the church, for the tranquillity of the world; for kings; for soldiers and allies; for the sick; for the afflicted; and, in a word, for all who stand in need of succor we supplicate and offer this Sacrifice.[26]

Thus Cyril's Church in Jerusalem believed that the Spirit of God still comes to his people, touches ordinary bread, and it becomes precious; by the power of the new Spirit wine is made the Blood of Christ. And after this great manifestation of God's glory, the very nature and perspective of the Christian fellowship is changed, seeking now and praying for peace in the Church, tranquillity in the world, and the well-being of others, from kings to the afflicted—in a word, praying for all who stand in need of succor, which is everybody.

The natural completion of these prayers and commemorations is the Lord's Prayer:

> Then, after these things, we say that Prayer which the Savior delivered to his own disciples, with a pure conscience styling God our Father, and saying, OUR FATHER, WHICH ART IN HEAVEN. O most surpassing loving-kindness of God! On them who revolted from him and were in the very extreme of misery has he bestowed such complete forgiveness of their evil deeds, and so great participation of grace, as that they should even call Him Father. "Our Father, which art in heaven"; they also, too, are a heaven who bear the image of the heavenly, in whom God is, *dwelling and walking in them* (II Cor. 6:16).[27]

So for Cyril, Jerusalem the old, holy hill of the Lord has become the new Jerusalem, where heaven itself is to be found in the worship of the people of God. The old temple may have been destroyed by one emperor and now a great basilica, built by another, may provide a magnificent setting for Christian worship, but what is decisive is the fact that each person can become God's holy hill, the inspiration point where God dwells and walks with his people.

Therefore it is appropriate that the liturgy should continue after the Lord's Prayer with these words:

> After this the priest says, HOLY THINGS TO HOLY PEOPLE. Holy are the gifts presented, since they have been visited by the Holy Ghost; holy are you also, having been vouchsafed the Holy Ghost; the holy things therefore correspond to the holy persons. Then you say, ONE IS HOLY, ONE IS THE LORD, JESUS CHRIST. For truly One is holy, by nature holy; we, too, are holy, but not by nature, only by participation, and discipline, and prayer. After this you hear the chanter, with a sacred melody inviting you to the communion of the Holy Mys-

teries, and saying, *O taste and see that the Lord is good* (Ps. 34:8).[28]

What the psalmist bade Israel do, was fulfilled at Jesus' Last Supper. And in the prayers of the early Church, the Lord's Supper continued the great heritage of Israel and united it with the ongoing worship of Jesus' companions, the new holy people of God, as they advanced through time and space to new mission and fellowship in his name.

Turning now to a final representative of the new, Christian Jerusalem in the worship of the Eastern Church, we come to Gregory of Nyssa. If in the Western Church we have found the treatise on the Lord's Prayer by Cyprian to be a more pastoral and devotional approach to the subject than the brilliance of his predecessor and teacher, a similar contrast may be drawn in Eastern Christianity between the profundity of Origen and the refreshing and delightful collection of five sermons by Gregory of Nyssa on the Lord's Prayer.

Born about 335, the year which saw the completion of the basilica in Jerusalem, Gregory devoted most of his life to theological reflection, preaching, and writing; he was Bishop of Nyssa, a small town in Cappadocia, now a region of eastern Turkey. Gregory was much indebted to the biblical studies of Origen and to the earlier traditions of Greek philosophy, his sermons achieving an impressive meeting of minds, both biblical and Platonic. In this friendly collaboration between the philosophy of Athens and the faith of Jerusalem, Gregory of Nyssa is an outstanding illustration of what Jerusalem could do with Athens (to use Tertullian's old antithesis) and how much benefit could be gained by mutual respect and courtesy.

Gregory's first sermon begins:

> The Divine Word teaches us the science of prayer. And to the disciples worthy of it, who eagerly asked to learn to pray in such a way as to win the favor of the Divine hearing, this science is proposed in the words that prayer should take. Now, I make bold to add a little to what Scripture says; for the present congregation needs instruction not so much on how to pray, as on the necessity of praying at all, a necessity that has perhaps not yet been grasped by most people. In fact, the majority of men grievously neglect in their life this sacred and divine work which is prayer.[29]

Gregory illustrates his point by speaking of shoppers who hasten, not to church but to the market for a bargain, the hour for prayer being usurped by other things that hold their interest. Or take the craftsman who thinks that prayer is lost time and divine assistance quite useless for the work he has in hand: "therefore he leaves prayer aside and places all his hopes in his hands, without remembering Him who has given him his hands."[30]

By the end of the first sermon, prayer seems so naturally appropriate to mankind, so preeminently reasonable and joyous an ascent to God, that only a fool would ignore such a precious treasure. The subsequent sermons are equally vivid and inspiring. For example, Gregory's comment on the beginning of the Lord's Prayer is as follows: "Our Father"

> means to remind you of our beautiful fatherland [in heaven]. And by thus putting into your mind a stronger desire for these good things, he sets you on the way that will lead you back to your original country.[31]

This theme of pilgrimage, God setting his own on their way to him, was of great importance for Abraham and Moses, Peter and Paul, Ignatius and Cyprian. To leave one's earthly fatherland for a promised land, even if with a long struggle for liberation or the bitter pain of martyrdom, is no loss if that journey takes you back to your original country, your true home with your Father in heaven.

It is, however, in Gregory's first sermon on the Beatitudes that we find the most remarkable synthesis of Greek piety and biblical faith. Gregory begins with a sermon text: "And seeing the multitudes, Jesus went up into a mountain . . ." (Mt 5:1). And to help his congregation pay attention to the words which open Jesus' Sermon on the Mount, Gregory begins with a question:

> Who among those present is a disciple of the Word, and sufficiently so to ascend with Him from the low ground —from superficial and ignoble thoughts to the spiritual mountain of sublime contemplation?[32]

What is this mountain of vision and contemplation, this inspiration point which is accessible to every disciple of Jesus Christ?

> This mountain leaves behind all shadows cast by the rising hills of wickedness; on the contrary, it is lit up on all sides by the rays of the true light, and from its summit all things that remain invisible to those imprisoned in the cave may be seen in the pure air of truth. Now the Word of God himself, who calls blessed those who have ascended with him, specifies the nature and number of the things that are contemplated from this height. He points them out, as it were, with his finger; here the Kingdom of heaven, there the inheritance of the earth that is

> above, then mercy, justice, consolation, kinship with the
> God of all creation, and the fruit of persecution, that is,
> to become a friend of God.[33]

Though we may still be lost in the cave, there is nonetheless
the true light, Jesus Christ, whose disciple and companion
we may become in the ascent to our true homeland. And
like Abraham of old, all of us may become friends of God.

> Since, then, the Lord ascends the mountain, let us listen
> to Isaiah who cries: *Come, let us go up to the mountain of the*
> *Lord* (Is.2:3). If we are weak through sin, let our feeble
> hands and weak knees be strengthened, as the prophet
> instructs us (Is.35:3). For when we have reached the sum-
> mit, we shall find Him who heals all illness and languor,
> who takes up our infirmities and bears our diseases
> (Is.53:4; Mt.8:17). Let us therefore ascend quickly, so
> that we may be established with Isaiah on the summit of
> hope and see from this vantage point the good things
> that the Word shows to those who follow Him to the
> heights.[34]

Here, some seven centuries after Plato wrote of the vision
from Delphi, traditional Greek piety has been baptized and
used by Gregory to help communicate the understanding
of worship and prayer he wishes to share with his Church.

And in his third sermon on the Beatitudes, Gregory
makes impressive use of Plato's theology found in the myth
of the cave, as he expounds the words of Jesus, "Blessed
are they that mourn":

> Let us take for an example two men living in a dark place,
> one of whom had been born in the dark, whilst the other
> had been used to enjoying the light outside and has

somehow been shut up in that place by force. Surely the present calamity will not affect both in the same way; for the man who knows of what he has been deprived will think the loss of light a very grave matter, whereas the one who does not know this gift at all will continue to live without sorrow. He will not think that he has lost anything worth having, because he has been brought up in darkness. . . . It is the same with the subject of our present meditation. If a man has been able to perceive the true good, and then realizes the poverty of human nature, he will certainly think the soul in distress. For he will consider that the present life is spent in sorrow, because it is removed from this true good. Therefore I would say that the Word does not call blessed the sorrow itself, but rather the realization of the good that produces this state of sorrow, which is due to the fact that the object of the desire is absent from our life.[35]

Indeed, blessed are they that mourn when their sorrow comes from a longing to enjoy and be with the Light of the World![36]

In conclusion, in the East, Gregory of Nyssa shows, in his sermons dealing with prayer and worship, that the inspiration points for Plato and the Old Testament writers are no longer private property, available to only an enlightened or chosen few. As Jesus himself taught, his disciples no longer worship God only on "this mountain," or in Jerusalem, "God's holy hill," for now is the hour when the Father is worshiped in spirit and in truth. Cyril, in the new Jerusalem, illustrates this new spirit of prayer in the great liturgy of his Church. Origen represents the new devotion to the Holy Bible as an unfailing light to illumine the paths of Jesus' disciples. And in the West, pagan Rome, the "harlot of Babylon," sitting on her seven hills drunk with the blood of the martyrs of Jesus (see Revelation 17f.), has fallen, for even in the dark catacombs where Christians had to live during the persecutions, their faith illuminated those caves and the surrounding darkness of ancient Rome with the Light of the World. And to the South, there is no longer the curse at the seashore by a mindless king against his hapless son, the dying Hippolytus, but instead the blessing of our Father in heaven upon his children along the shores of the Mediterranean, where Tertullian, Cyprian, and Origen made known to their companions the riches of the Lord's Prayer. Finally to the North and beyond lay the frontier for the ancient world, with nations yet to be born, baptized, and confirmed with the Spirit of Christ. In the ongoing worship of the Church and in the deepening of individual Christian prayer and personal commitment, inspiration points have become in number like the sands of the seashore; a galaxy of mountaintop experiences are our heritage. The words of Isaiah were never more significant: "Come, let us go up to the mountain of the Lord." That inspiration point is near us because the Lord is near us, indeed in our midst, wherever we are. Come let us adore him!

THEMES FOR REFLECTION AND DISCUSSION

1. In this chapter we have moved from the world of the Bible to that of the early Church. Do you feel comfortable in this later atmosphere, even though you may find yourself more at home with biblical writers? Or do you have a dislike for the postbiblical period? Think what your preferences can tell you about your own point of view and basic assumptions. On the other hand, the Fathers of the Church may seem to you far more human and approachable than

the figures in the Bible. Again, reflection upon your attitude can help you recognize your own agenda when you try to encounter and communicate with other Christians in different times and places. One of the delights of contemporary biblical and patristic scholarship is the close collaboration and sense of fellowship shared by Catholic and Protestant students. We are learning much from each other, and with much mutual pleasure and encouragement.

2. Throughout our study we have omitted the title *Saint,* traditionally prefaced to the names of the apostles and other great and holy persons in the Bible and in the subsequent history of the Church, simply to economize space and to express a simplicity in Christian style when possible. Paul referred to his readers repeatedly as "the saints," a term applied to all the faithful in Christ, who are "called to be saints" (1 Cor 1:2; 2 Cor 1:1). St. Peter and St. Paul, not to mention St. Ignatius of Antioch or St. Cyprian of Carthage, were given their titles in recognition of their preeminent sanctity and power for good in the life of the Church. The idea of sainthood and holiness is an important motif in the Bible and Church history. It is a reminder that the Christian life presupposes a pilgrimage, progress toward a goal, fulfillment of a vocation. Consider your own sense of calling, where you are now, and what you hope to accomplish in the coming days. *Quo vadis?* Where are you going?

3. A frequent theme in our study has been an understanding of prayer as growth, increasingly upward in closeness to God and outward as it embraces more and more persons in community and affection. An illustration from geometry may be helpful. The equilateral triangle reaches up higher as its base becomes broader; conversely, its outreach becomes more widespread as its peak ascends. Worship in our language grew out of the Old English *weorthscipe,*

worth-ship, creating worth, honorableness, dignity. Our worship grows geometrically as we recognize and respond to the worth, honor, and dignity both of our Creator and his creation, the people with whom we live, work, and play. Worship of God means, in the splendid attitude of John Wesley, looking upon all the world as our parish.

OPTIONAL LENTEN STUDY GUIDE

1. The Collect for the Sunday of the Passion, Palm Sunday, introduces Holy Week, the last week of Lent:

> Almighty and everliving God, in your tender love for the human race you sent your Son our Savior Jesus Christ to take upon him our nature, and to suffer death upon the cross, giving us the example of his great humility: Mercifully grant that we may walk in the way of his suffering, and also share in his resurrection; through Jesus Christ our Lord, who lives and reigns with you and the Holy Spirit, one God, for ever and ever.[37]

This ancient collect, stemming ultimately from the prayer book of Gregory the Great, speaks of our walking in the way of Christ's suffering, a reference which recalls the custom of Cyril's Church in Jerusalem to gather on the Mount of Olives on each Palm Sunday to trace the way Jesus took to enter Jerusalem. Pope Gregory (590–604) is well-known in the English-speaking world for sending Augustine as a missionary to Canterbury as its first archbishop. This prayer is thus an impressive reminder of the richness of our common Christian heritage.[38] Our Lord gave his Church the example of his great humility during the first Holy Week. Many of his earliest disciples suffered death for his sake. The Eastern Church followed his footsteps year by year on Palm

Sunday. The Western Church extended the custom, and one of its greatest popes inspired an outstanding missionary to proclaim Christ far across the northern frontiers in ongoing companionship with the risen Lord.

2. Gregory the Great is also the author of the famous Lenten hymn, *Audi, benigne conditor:*

> Kind Maker of the world O hear
>> The fervent prayer, with many a tear
> Poured forth by all the penitent
>> Who keep this holy fast of Lent!
> Each heart is manifest to thee;
>> Thou knowest our infirmity;
> Now we repent, and seek thy face;
>> Grant unto us thy pardoning grace.[39]

Gregory's profound hymn, sung for centuries by countless numbers of Christian communities throughout the West, expresses the earnestness and devotion which is especially appropriate to the beginning of Holy Week, a piety and sense of commitment characteristic of the many martyrs who preceded him during the fiery ordeals of Roman persecution. Christ's pardoning grace came through his cross, and the way of the cross, humility, and suffering is the way Christ chose to reach the glory of his resurrection. The great Lutheran pastor, Dietrich Bonhoeffer, a martyr during the Nazi persecution, was to express very similar ideas when he wrote of the high cost of discipleship, in contrast to "cheap" (that is, pseudo) grace.[40]

3. Palm Sunday marks the beginning of the most solemn week of Lent, which goes on to the commemoration of the Last Supper on Maundy Thursday, the deep contrition and unfathomable intensity of Good Friday, the quiet prepara-

tion of Holy Saturday, leading up to the joyous celebration of Easter. Even though Good Friday lies ahead, with its remembrance of Christ's suffering and death upon the cross, the Collect for Palm Sunday sees, along with the way of Christ's suffering, the goal of his resurrection. This balance between the death of Friday and the new life of Sunday is a recurring theme in our worship; as Francis of Assisi was to say, it is in dying that we are born to eternal life.[41] Gregory of Nyssa claimed that our Lord's beatitude about the blessedness of those who mourn is to be understood as his blessing upon our sorrow and longing for the good now absent from our lives. Good Friday is indeed good because it shows us the absence of our greatest Good and makes us seek more and more for the joy of his presence.

NOTES AND SUGGESTIONS
FOR FURTHER READING

CHAPTER I
WORSHIP IN ANCIENT GREECE

1. Among Christian writers indebted to the Greek heritage of the Church, Paul himself quotes from two Greek poets, according to Acts 17. The Gospel of John and the Epistle to the Hebrews both make use of Greek philosophical reflection. And in the early Church, Justin Martyr has a high regard for Socrates, who exhorted "men by meditation to learn more about God who was unknown to them" (*Second Apology*, 10), translated by Thomas B. Falls, *Saint Justin Martyr* (New York: Christian Heritage, Inc., 1948), p. 130.

2. A convenient selection of the writings of Plato dealing with his teacher, Socrates, has been translated, with a brief introduction, by Hugh Tredennick, *Plato: The Last Days of Socrates* (Harmondsworth: Penguin Books, 1959). The quotation comes from the *Apology*, 21ff. (Penguin text, p. 50ff.).

3. E. A. Blackburn has compiled an outstanding anthology of devotional readings entitled *A Treasury of the Kingdom* (London: Oxford University Press, 1954). He calls the first part of his work "The Approach to the Kingdom," and quotes from the *Apology of Socrates* as a "forerunner" to the kingdom, p. 5f. This version, which he has condensed and slightly simplified, was made in 1892 by Benjamin Jowett, the famous

Master of Balliol College, Oxford, whose translations of Plato are among the most beautiful in English.

4. The translation is by H. D. P. Lee, *Plato: The Republic* (Harmondsworth: Penguin Books, 1955), VII: 515ff., (p. 279ff.). Lee has a valuable introduction, and his brief section on philosophy and religion (p. 35f.) is especially interesting. For example, he suggests that for Plato "the ultimate objective of . . . philosophic training is religious. . . ." For further discussion of Socrates' religious vocation, see A. E. Taylor's *Socrates: The Man and His Thought* (Garden City, New York: Doubleday, 1956), especially p. 44ff. and pp. 77–82.

5. Adam Fox, a former colleague of C. S. Lewis at Magdalen College, Oxford, has written a delightful study, *Plato and the Christians* (London: SCM Press, 1957). There is a fascinating section on prayer, from which this illustration is taken, *Phaedrus* 279B–C (p. 188).

6. *Ibid., Laws* 712B (p. 186).

7. *Ibid., Timaeus* 27C (p. 185f.).

8. *Ibid., Laws* 687–688A (p. 184f.).

9. Euripides, "Hippolytus" translated by David Grene in *The Complete Greek Tragedies* (1955), V, edited by David Grene and Richmond Lattimore (New York: The Modern Library), copyright, 1942, by The University of Chicago. Reprinted by permission. The citation comes from Scene III (pp. 205, 207f.).

10. Andre-Jean Festugiere suggests that the devotion Hippolytus had for Artemis may be compared to the dedication felt by a medieval knight for the Virgin Mary. See his valuable lectures published as *Personal Religion Among the Greeks* (Berkeley: University of California Press, 1954), p. 15.

11. *Hippolytus*, V (p. 216ff.).

12. *Ibid.*, Epilogue (p. 233).

13. *Ibid.* (p. 238f.).

14. For reference, the hymn is found, for example, in the *Hymnal of the Protestant Episcopal Church* (New York: The Church Pension Fund, 1940), 376. The full Italian text with an additional stanza in English is found in the exceptionally valuable *The Hymnal 1940 Companion,* Third Edition (New York: The Church Pension Fund, 1951).

15. Episcopal *Hymnal,* 419.

16. The Proposed Book of Common Prayer (New York: The Seabury Press, 1977), p. 218.

17. Episcopal *Hymnal,* 542.

18. The two hymns face each other in the Episcopal *Hymnal*, 60 and 61.

CHAPTER II
ABRAHAM AND MOSES IN THE WORSHIP OF ISRAEL

1. This question is discussed by Tertullian, *The Prescription Against Heretics*, VII, in, for example, *The Ante-Nicene Fathers*, III, edited by Alexander Roberts and James Donaldson (Buffalo: The Christian Literature Publishing Company, 1887), p. 246.

2. A. S. Herbert has published a helpful monograph, *Worship in Ancient Israel* (Richmond, Virginia: John Knox Press, 1959). A. Hamman, *Prayer: The New Testament* (Chicago: Franciscan Herald Press, 1971) has an invaluable first part entitled "The Biblical Basis of Christian Prayer," a fifty-nine page survey of the Old Testament background.

3. The idea of obedience is of fundamental importance for the biblical understanding of worship. See, for example, the attractive article on this topic by W. A. Whitehouse in *A Theological Word Book of the Bible*, edited by Alan Richardson (New York: The Macmillan Company, 1953), p. 160f.

4. Gerhard Von Rad, *Genesis* (London: SCM Press, 1961), pp. 206–209.

5. Soren Kierkegaard's *Fear and Trembling*, translated by Walter Lowrie (Princeton: The University Press, 1941), is a profound study of the sacrifice of Isaac, and would provide an excellent introduction to the thought of this nineteenth-century Danish philosopher, whose writings have had great influence upon contemporary theology.

6. An unforgettable example of the evil of child sacrifice in the Greek tradition is found in Aeschylus' three tragedies, the *Oresteia*. Compare the grim story of Jephthah's daughter in Judges 11.

7. Gerhard Von Rad has written an attractive introduction to the life and teaching of Moses, published in the valuable series, *World Christian Books;* it is entitled *Moses* (New York: Association Press, n.d.).

8. Cited by Adam Fox, *Plato and the Christians*, p. 11.

9. The most ancient traditions about the establishment of the Passover are probably to be found in Exodus 12:21–27. The excerpts cited come from verses 3, 6ff., 11ff., 21, 24f., and 27. For an excellent summary of the complicated development of traditions in the Old Testament dealing with the Passover, see L. H. Brockington's lucid discussion in Hasting's *Dictionary of the Bible*, revised by F. C. Grant and H. H.

Rowley (New York: Charles Scribner's Sons, 1963), p. 729f.

10. Raphael Posner, Uri Kaploun, and Shalom Cohen have edited a beautiful book, *Jewish Liturgy: Prayer and Synagogue Service Through the Ages* (New York: Leon Amiel Publisher, 1975). See pp. 143–146 for their main discussion of the Passover. For further reading the entire book is of great interest, especially the very attractive section on the Day of Atonement, the "Sabbath of Sabbaths," the "Holiest day of the year" (pp. 173–183).

11. See the regulations in Deuteronomy 16 for centralizing the Passover in Jerusalem.

12. See John 2:13, 11:55, and Luke 22:7. To this day the date for the Christian celebration of Easter is determined by using the ancient Jewish method of reckoning the date of Passover.

13. The celebration of a Seder supper for Christians is becoming increasingly popular as a way of sharing in the faith and hopes of Israel, our "elder brother." This community meal is particularly meaningful if it is observed in churches one week before the Maundy Thursday liturgy, as a preparation for the commemoration of Jesus' own Passover at the Last Supper.

14. The 1928 edition, p. 17.

15. See especially verses 8, 23, and 28f.

16. The Proposed Book of Common Prayer, p. 218.

17. Found, for example, in the Episcopal *Hymnal,* 563.

CHAPTER III
THE PRAYERS OF DAVID AND SOLOMON

1. Two excellent examples of a Christian approach to the Psalter would include George D. Carleton's *The English Psalter With a Devotional Commentary* (London: A. R. Mowbray, 1945), and C. S. Lewis, *Reflections on the Psalms* (London: Geoffrey Bles, 1958).

2. G. W. Anderson has written a valuable concise commentary on the psalms, published in *Peake's Commentary on the Bible,* revised and edited by Matthew Black and H. H. Rowley (London: Nelson, 1962), pp. 409–443. This one-volume commentary on the entire Bible provides an outstanding survey of modern scholarship. A more recent single volume commentary has been edited by Raymond E. Brown, Joseph A. Fitzmyer, and Roland E. Murphy, *The Jerome Biblical Commentary* (Englewood Cliffs, New Jersey: Prentice-Hall, 1968); it also has a valuable section on the Psalter, pp. 569–602.

3. Compare the text of this version with that cited on p. 33 from the Revised Standard Version. An excellent new version of the Bible has recently appeared, entitled the *Good News Bible* (New York: The American Bible Society, 1976). Psalm 1 is translated in this version with these opening words: "Happy are those who reject the advice of evil men, who do not follow the example of sinners or join those who have no use for God. Instead, they find joy in obeying the Law of the Lord, and they study it day and night."

4. James Wood's *Wisdom Literature: An Introduction* (London: Duckworth, 1967) offers an attractive survey of wisdom in the ancient world, and particularly in the Bible. His comments on Solomon's wisdom are very helpful, pp. 47–51. Compare Walter Brueggemann's fascinating *In Man We Trust: The Neglected Side of Biblical Faith* (Richmond, Virginia: John Knox Press, 1972), especially chapter 4, which deals with the period from Saul to Solomon, and chapter 6, "The Wise Man as a Model for Ministry."

5. An exceptionally beautiful and perceptive Jewish study of prayer, drawing deeply both from biblical and rabbinical piety, and from contemporary intellectual reflection on the subject, is Abraham Joshua Heschel's *Man's Quest for God: Studies in Prayer and Symbolism* (New York: Charles Scribner's Sons, 1954). See especially chapter 2, "The Person and the Word."

6. An outstanding and pioneering study of the theological implications of femininity in the Bible was written by Margaret E. Thrall, *The Ordination of Women to the Priesthood* (London: SCM Press, 1958).

7. The Proposed Book of Common Prayer, p. 218. This prayer is also found in the *Service Book and Hymnal* of the Lutheran Church (Minneapolis: Augsburg Publishing House, 1958), p. 84, and in the *Book of Worship for Church and Home* (Nashville, Tennessee: The Methodist Publishing House, 1964), p. 95.

8. Episcopal *Hymnal,* 2; see also *The Hymnal 1940 Companion.*

CHAPTER IV
LUKE'S PICTURE OF PRAYER
AND MATTHEW'S ACCOUNT OF THE LORD'S PRAYER

1. For a valuable discussion of all the New Testament evidence, see Donald Coggan, *The Prayers of the New Testament* (New York: Harper and Row, 1967). In this work, the Archbishop of Canterbury presents the

prayers of the New Testament in both the King James and the New English Bible translations, with excellent commentary.

2. On the titles applied to Jesus, see Sherman Johnson, *The Theology of the Gospels* (London: Duckworth, 1966), especially pp. 163–172. Reginald H. Fuller has published a companion volume, *A Critical Introduction to the New Testament* (London: Duckworth, 1971) which offers an invaluable survey of the formation of the New Testament writings. These two volumes are highly recommended for further study.

3. Joachim Jeremias, *New Testament Theology, Volume I: The Proclamation of Jesus* (London: SCM Press, 1971), p. 198 stresses the importance of the Kaddish as the background of the Lord's Prayer. The text of the Kaddish cited here is probably the most ancient form current biblical research can determine. A modern form of the Kaddish is found in the *Union Prayerbook for Jewish Worship* (Cincinnati: The Central Conference of American Rabbis, 1940), p. 71.

4. John V. Taylor, *The Go-Between God* (London: SCM Press, 1972), p. 225. It is also cited in *The Fourth Lesson in the Daily Office, Book II,* edited by Christopher Campling (London: Darton, Longman & Todd, 1974), p. 295, an outstanding recent anthology of meditative readings to accompany prayer.

5. Philip B. Harner, *Understanding the Lord's Prayer* (Philadelphia: Fortress Press, 1975) is an admirable and thorough study of recent research on the Lord's Prayer.

6. The Proposed Book of Common Prayer, p. 219. *The* [Presbyterian] *Worshipbook* (Philadelphia: The Westminster Press, 1970), p. 143, provides a Lenten Collect which expresses a similar theme from the Gospel of John, that of Jesus as God's Living Water for a thirsty mankind. It begins: "God of holy love: you have poured out living water in the gift of your Son Jesus."

CHAPTER V
THE OLD TEMPLE AND THE NEW SPIRIT
OF PRAYER FOR PETER AND PAUL

1. John V. Taylor's *The Go-Between God* (London: SCM Press, 1972) is a fine study of the Holy Spirit and mission in the life of the Church today.

2. Citing the *Septuagint,* the Greek translation of the Old Testament.

3. Compare Genesis 11:1–9 with Acts 2:1–11.

4. Michael Grant, *Saint Paul* (New York: Charles Scribner's Sons,

1976) is a stimulating study of the apostle and the world in which he lived. See also D. M. Stanley, *Boasting in the Lord* (New York: Paulist Press, 1973), which is a thorough and helpful study of prayer in the life and thought of Paul.

5. Louis Bouyer has written an outstanding study entitled *Eucharist* (Notre Dame, Indiana: The University Press, 1968); in chapters 2, 3, 4, and 5 he particularly stresses the close ties between Jewish thanksgivings and liturgy, and the Christian Eucharist.

6. The Proposed Book of Common Prayer, p. 219.

7. Hymn 263 in the Episcopal *Hymnal*. See the *Companion* to the *Hymnal* for further interesting details about the history and use of this great hymn.

CHAPTER VI
THE ADVANCE OF CHRISTIAN FAITH
AND WORSHIP IN THE WEST AND IN THE EAST

1. An excellent brief account of prayer in the *Apostolic Fathers* is given by Eric George Jay in part I of his book, *Origen's Treatise on Prayer* (London: SPCK, 1954); see especially pp. 6–12.

2. The *Apostolic Fathers,* translated by Kirsopp Lake in the Loeb Classical Library (Cambridge, Massachusetts: Harvard University Press, 1952), Vol. I, pp. 195ff.

3. Ignatius, *Epistle to the Romans* (Loeb edition, pp. 227ff.).

4. There are other writings from the *Apostolic Fathers* which illustrate prayer in the early Church. See, for example, the Epistle of Bishop Clement of Rome, writing in A.D. 96, especially *I Clement* 38 and 53 (Loeb text, vol. I, p. 73ff. and p. 99ff.). Bishop Polycarp of Smyrna, martyred in the year 155, has a fine prayer for the Philippians in his letter to them (ch. 12; Loeb text, vol. I, p. 299); compare the later "Martyrdom of Polycarp," which describes his lengthy prayer before his death (Loeb text, vol. II, p. 319, p. 331ff.). An important early Church manual dealing with Christian conduct and worship is known as the *Didache,* or "The Lord's Teaching to the Heathen by the Twelve Apostles." In this fascinating work, which may be as old as some of the New Testament writings, prayer is mentioned several times, the Lord's Prayer is cited, and instruction is given concerning baptism and the Eucharist (Loeb text, vol. I, p. 309–333, especially p. 321ff. and p. 331.).

5. The *Writings of Saint Justin Martyr,* published in the series entitled

Mountain and Wilderness

The Fathers of the Church (New York: Christian Heritage, Inc., 1948), offers a convenient text for further study of Justin. Note, for example, his appreciation of Greek and Jewish piety: Christ "is the Word of whom all mankind partakes. Those who lived by reason are Christians, even though they have been considered atheists: such as, among the Greeks, Socrates, Heraclitus, and others like them; and among the foreigners, Abraham, Elias . . ." *First Apology,* 46 (p. 83). See also section 13 (p. 45f.) dealing with prayer and hymns. *I Apology* 65ff. (pp.104–107) gives a picture of Christian worship and the Eucharist; and his *Dialogue with Trypho* 35 (p. 201f.) and 96 (p. 299f.) deal with prayer for one's enemies.

6. A valuable excerpt from the *Passion of SS Perpetua and Felicitas,* describing their worship and prayers just prior to their death, is found in E. G. Jay, *Origen's Treatise on Prayer,* p. 18ff.

7. Ernest Evans, *Tertullian's Tract on the Prayer* (London: SPCK, 1953), section 1 (p. 3).

8. See our earlier discussion at the beginning of Chapter two.

9. *On the Prayer,* section 10 (p. 17); see also sections 11, 13, 16, and 25.

10. *Ibid.,* section 29 (p. 39ff.).

11. See the introduction by Roy F. Deferrari to the treatise on *The Lord's Prayer,* in *Saint Cyprian: Treatises* (New York: Fathers of the Church, Inc., 1958), p. 125.

12. *The Lord's Prayer,* chapters 2 and 8 (p. 128, 132).

13. *Ibid.,* chapter 11 (p. 136).

14. The primary source for the destruction of Jerusalem is Josephus' *The Jewish War.* See also Kathleen M. Kenyon, *Digging Up Jerusalem* (New York: Praeger, 1974).

15. See Charles Coüasnon, *The Church of the Holy Sepulchre in Jerusalem* (London: Oxford University Press, 1974), p. 12.

16. *The Oxford Dictionary of the Christian Church,* edited by F. L. Cross and E. A. Livingstone (London: Oxford University Press, 1974), has an outstanding selection of articles on these cities and the persons we are discussing, many of which would provide valuable additional reading and helpful bibliography.

17. The quotation is from E. G. Jay's admirable book, *Origen's Treatise on Prayer,* section I,1 (p. 79); compare section XXXIV (p. 218f.), the ending of his *Treatise.*

18. A prayer of Origen for guidance in his discussion of prayer is found at II,6 (p. 88).

19. *On Prayer,* II,1f. (p. 82f.).

20. Jay cites nearly two hundred references in Origen's *Treatise* to passages from the Old Testament, and some 230 citations from the New Testament, many of which are discussed more than once—a striking example of how exceptionally Bible-orientated is Origen's work.

21. *On Prayer,* XXXIII,1 (p. 216f.).

22. Charles Coüasnon, *The Church of the Holy Sepulchre in Jerusalem,* p. 14ff.

23. By the time of the Council of Chalcedon in 451, the Bishop of Jerusalem was declared to be a patriarch of the Church.

24. F. L. Cross has edited St. Cyril of Jerusalem's *Lectures on the Christian Sacraments* (London: SPCK, 1951) and in his excellent introduction has a brief survey of liturgy in Jerusalem, p. xix and following.

25. *Procatechesis,* 16f. The translation is by William Tefler, who edited *Cyril of Jerusalem and Nemesius of Emesa,* volume IV of the *Library of Christian Classics* (London: SCM Press, 1955), p. 76.

26. *Mystagogical Catecheses,* V,7f. (edition of Cross, p. 74). The translation is by the nineteenth-century Anglican scholar, R. W. Church, Dean of St. Paul's Cathedral, 1871–1890. I have modernized his spellings slightly.

27. *Ibid.,* V,11 (p. 75).

28. *Ibid.,* V,19f. (p. 78f.). I make a small correction in Dean Church's translation of the Greek *hagiois.*

29. Hilda C. Graef, *St. Gregory of Nyssa: The Lord's Prayer* and *The Beatitudes,* volume 18 of *Ancient Christian Writers* (Westminster, Maryland: The Newman Press, 1954), p. 21.

30. *Ibid.,* p. 22.

31. *Ibid.,* p. 42.

32. *Ibid.,* p. 85.

33. *Ibid.* See Plato's myth of the cave, p. 11ff. above.

34. *Ibid.,* p. 86. On Abraham as God's friend, see p. 27 above.

35. *Ibid.,* p. 110.

36. Two other theologians of the early Eastern Church have important writings on the Lord's Prayer. John Chrysostom, Bishop of Constantinople, preached a series of sermons based upon the Sermon on the Mount.

His homily XIX deals with the Lord's Prayer, and is an exquisite example of this "golden-mouthed" preacher, which is what *chrysostom* means in Greek. See Jaroslav Pelikan, *The Preaching of Chrysostom* (Philadelphia: Fortress Press, 1967). Also important is the commentary on the Lord's Prayer by Chrysostom's friend, Theodore of Mopsuestia. It is published in the series *Woodbrook Studies VI* (Cambridge: Heffer, 1933).

37. The Proposed Book of Common Prayer, p. 219. The prayer is also used on Palm Sunday in the Lutheran *Service Book and Hymnal,* p. 86, and in the Roman Catholic *Sacramentary:* The Roman Missal revised by decree of the Second Vatican Council and published by authority of Pope Paul VI (New York: Catholic Book Publishing Co., 1974), p. 126.

38. Massey H. Shepherd, Jr., *The Oxford American Prayer Book Commentary* (New York: Oxford University Press, 1950) has fascinating details and historical background for this Collect.

39. The full text is in the Episcopal *Hymnal,* 56. See the corresponding discussion in *The Hymnal, 1940, Companion* (New York: The Church Pension Fund, 1951).

40. See, for example, Dietrich Bonhoeffer, *The Cost of Discipleship,* first published in 1937.

41. A fine updated version of the prayer of St. Francis is found in The Proposed Book of Common Prayer, p.833.